THE
DAYNE
GAME

THE
DAYNE GAME

*Ron Dayne and the Greatest Day in
Wisconsin Football History*

JUSTIN DOHERTY

Cataloging-in-Publication Data is available from the Library of Congress.

First KCI Sports Publishing edition: 2009
ISBN-13: 978-0-9798729-9-0
ISBN-10: 0-9798729-9-5

Book Layout and Design: Nicky Brillowski

This book is available in quantity at special discounts for your group or organization. For further information, contact:

KCI Sports Publishing
3340 Whiting Avenue
Suite 5
Stevens Point, WI 54481
(217) 766-3390
Fax: (715) 344-2668

Photos courtesy of: AP Images, University of Wisconsin Athletic Communications, Madison Capital Times, Danielle Dirienzo, Heisman Trophy Trust.

CONTENTS

Contents v

Dedication vi

Acknowledgements vii

Foreword   Ron Dayne ix

Preface 12

1   Setting the Wheels in Motion 16

2   Recruiting Ron Dayne 21

3   On to Wisconsin 27

4   The Freshman Phenom 34

5   The Great Dayne 63

6   The Road to the Roses 91

7   Run For the Record 107

8   Perfection 139

9   The Heisman 198

Ron Dayne Statistics 209

Bibliography 216

DEDICATION

To the fans who held up
the towels and the team
that gave them reason to do so.

ACKNOWLEDGEMENTS

Dozens of people contributed, in a variety of ways, to this book. Thank you to …

My wife, Martha, and my daughter, Erin, for their support and patience as I spent hours and hours at home interviewing, writing and editing. They're the Heisman winners in our house.

Ron and Alia Dayne, Steve Malchow, Matt Lepay, Barry Alvarez, John Chadima and my wife, Martha, for reading the manuscript and making valuable suggestions and edits. Their feedback was very important to me.

The following 82 people for graciously giving me some of their time for interviews or background information. The final product is largely a result of what they provided to me. Thanks to:

Barry Alvarez, Neil Ament, Andy Baggot, Laura Behnke, Luke Behnke, Glenn Betts, Bret Bielema, Brooks Bollinger, Tim Brandt, Chuck Bruhn, John Chadima, Tim Chatman, Chris Chambers, Tim Condon, Jon Corl, Dave Costa, Anthony Davis, Nick Davis, Alia Dayne, Onya Dayne, Ron Dayne, Russ Dengel, John Dettmann, Dannielle DiRienzo, Brian Ebner, Wayne Esser, Scott Faulkner, Kirk Ferentz, Bill Ferrario, Alan Fish, Vern Fowler, Barry Fox, Butch Gebhardt, Chris Ghidorzi, Leslie Gudel, Joe Hart, Patrick Herb, Ben Herbert, Ed Hopkins, Jim Hueber, Jeffrey Jaffe, Daron Jones, Scott Kavanagh, Kevin Kluender, Jay Koritzinsky, Chad Kuhns, Matt Lepay, Judy Lowell, Mike Mahnke, Steve Malchow, Bill Marek, Cecil Martin, Henry Mason, Mike McComiskey, Skip McGregor, Chris McIntosh, Terry Murawski, Rick Nelson, Todd Nelson, Mark Peeler, Kevin Phelps, Deb Piper, Casey Rabach, Brenda Reid, Rob Reid, Pat Richter, Rob Roell, Dave Santek, Steve

Sasso, Craig Schreiner, Jim Steffenhagen, Vince Sweeney, Donnel Thompson, Doug Tiedt, Matt Unertl, Mike Unitan, Robb Vogel, Robert Vowels, Brian White, Jay Wilson, Bernie Wyatt, Jake Zimmerman.

Finally, to Peter Clark of KCI Sports Publishing for partnering with me on this project.

FOREWORD

I t's crazy to me that it's been 10 years already.

Playing football at Wisconsin was a special time for me. It seems like yesterday when I played my last game in Camp Randall Stadium. The game against Iowa, the final regular-season game my senior year, everything on the line, man, how could it have ended any better? What a great day.

The two Big Ten and Rose Bowl championship teams we had at Wisconsin in 1998 and 1999 were amazing. We had great coaches. And the team, we were great teammates and great friends. We had a lot of talented guys on the team.

I've got to give props to my line. We had the best offensive line. Without them leading the way, I would never have set the record and won the Heisman. Manny, Vandy, Derek, Jerry, Macky, Gibby, Babyface, Bill, Casey, Dave. We were a tight team and I still consider them all my friends.

My final game against Iowa in '99 was something I'll never forget. It's an honor for me to have my name up inside the stadium. I still can't believe none of us saw it while we were practicing that week! During the postgame ceremony, when I saw it for the first time, I didn't know what to do. I was shocked. When they gave me the mic, I remember telling the fans, "thanks, I love you all." I thought I was going to get another chance to say something, but I didn't get the mic back. I have the chance now to tell you what I was going to say ...

I want all the Wisconsin fans to know how much I appreciate

the support they gave me and the team. One of the best decisions I made was to come to Wisconsin and play in front of the best fans in college football. Everyone – from the students to the alumni to the people in Madison and all over Wisconsin – made football Saturdays special. And thanks to my teammates and coaches (especially Coach Alvy, Coach Wyatt and Coach White). I couldn't have done it without you.

I hope you enjoy this book. It's a good look back at a special time in my life and a special time for my teammates, coaches and all Badger fans.

-Ron Dayne

"There comes a time when all the cosmic tumblers have clicked into place and the universe opens itself up for a few seconds to show you what's possible."

-Ray Kinsella, quoting author Terrance Mann, in "Field of Dreams"

PREFACE

They're like codes of some kind. The "Miracle on Ice." The "Immaculate Reception." Or – closer to home – "The Ice Bowl." They aren't the official names for these legendary sporting moments. Rather, popularized by fans and media over time, they are nicknames that have come to actually identify those events. It's not necessary to refer to them by formal names like 1980 Winter Olympics, 1972 AFC Divisional Playoff or 1967 NFL Championship game.

Similarly, mention "The Dayne Game" to any Wisconsin football fan and he or she will know exactly what you're talking about. No further explanation is needed. It was a day like no other in the history of Badger athletics and, for those who bleed Cardinal and White and were inside Camp Randall Stadium on that unseasonably warm November afternoon in 1999, it was an experience they will never forget.

I can remember when I first mentioned to Barry Alvarez that I was thinking about writing a book about the day that Ron Dayne broke the NCAA rushing record against Iowa. He asked, "How can you write a book about just one game?" It was a fair question. Looking back, I'm not even sure how well I had thought it out. What I knew, however, was that for the past 10 years I got chills whenever I thought about, spoke about or watched a video clip of that game. In particular, the image of thousands and thousands of white towels waving in unison from the hands of Badger fans as they celebrated the culmination of a remarkable season – and the singular accomplishment of a once-in-a-generation player – continues to mesmerize me a decade after it happened. I guess I figured I'm probably not alone.

The rags-to-riches story of Wisconsin athletics in the 1990s had, in many ways, already been completed by 1999, Dayne's senior season. Donna Shalala, who came to the Madison campus as the school's chancellor in 1988, had decided that the UW's moribund intercollegiate athletics program – specifically its football and men's basketball teams – should be just as competitive as the university's renowned academic departments. Shalala reached back into Wisconsin's last really successful era in football – the early 1960s – and hired Pat Richter, who had grown up on the east side of Madison, was a three-sport star at the UW and went on to a nine-year career in the National Football League. He was working as an executive at Oscar Mayer Corp. in Madison when Shalala convinced him to return to campus as director of athletics and resuscitate the sports program at his alma mater.

Knowing that the success of UW athletics depended on the success of the football program, Richter hired Barry Alvarez, Notre Dame's defensive coordinator and assistant head coach, to guide the fortunes of Badger football. Alvarez had always been associated with winning program – as a linebacker at Nebraska, a high school coach, an assistant coach at Iowa under Hayden Fry and, at Notre Dame, where he helped lead head coach Lou Holtz's Fighting Irish to the 1988 national championship and a three-year record (1987-89) of 32-5. Alvarez exuded confidence, enthusiasm and a no-nonsense attitude – three characteristics that were sorely lacking in the Badger football program at the time. Alvarez even had the nerve to offer advice to Badger fans during his introductory press conference: "They better get season tickets now, because before long they won't be able to." In 1984, Wisconsin had averaged a then school record 74,681 fans per game, but five years later that number had plummeted to just 41,734, the school's lowest average since 1945 when Camp Randall's capacity was 30,000 less than 1989's 76,293.

Alvarez's program turnaround is one of the great stories not only in the history of Wisconsin athletics, but in Big Ten and national college football annals as well. He took a program that had won a total of six games from 1987 to 1989 and by New Year's Day of 1994, had won the school's first Big Ten title since 1962 and turned the Rose Bowl into "Camp Randall West." The Badgers punctuated the program's resurrection that day with a 21-16 victory over UCLA.

Many of the team's stars from the magical 1993 season were set to return the following year and Wisconsin entered its 1994 season opener against Eastern Michigan with its highest preseason Associated Press ranking – 10th – since 1963. But injuries, off-the-field incidents and what Alvarez has called a "lack of continuity" all combined to prevent Wisconsin from returning to its lofty position of a year earlier. Nonetheless, the Badgers finished with wins in four of their last five games, including a 34-20 victory over 25th-ranked Duke in the Hall of Fame Bowl on New Year's Day. But by 1995, practically the entire starting lineup from the conference championship team of two years prior had turned over. The Badgers lost 43-7 at home to 13th-ranked Colorado in the season opener and despite a 17-9 win at No. 6 Penn State in September, ended the year with just one win in November and spent the holidays at home for the first time since 1992.

The loss that eliminated the Badgers from the bowl scene in 1995 was a 33-20 setback at home against Iowa on November 18. Wisconsin, with starting tailback Carl McCullough out of the lineup due to a shoulder injury, rushed for minus 18 yards. The Badgers' leading rusher in the game was Aaron Stecker, who carried 13 times for 25 yards. Wisconsin finished the 1995 season ranked 10th in the Big Ten in rushing yards per game after having the conference's top ground game just two years earlier. The Badgers needed to re-establish the punishing running attack that had spearheaded their rise to prominence, and they needed a tail-back who could help them do that. They found one in Ron Dayne, who decided to attend Wisconsin on his visit to campus the week-end of the 1995 Iowa game. That decision helped set in motion a sequence of events that would lead four years later to the most magical day in the history of Camp Randall Stadium.

Ron Dayne, of course, was the focal point of the Wisconsin-Iowa game on November 13, 1999. He had stayed at Wisconsin for his senior year and was now on the cusp of eclipsing the NCAA career rushing record set by Texas' Ricky Williams in 1998. Dayne had also put himself in position to become Wisconsin's first Heisman Trophy winner since 1954. The Badger football program, which had won the 1998 Big Ten title and the 1999 Rose Bowl, now had the opportunity to clinch another conference champi-onship, become the first Big Ten school ever to win Rose Bowls in back-to-back seasons and prove that its resurgence earlier in the decade was no fluke. The "Dayne Game" is also about Wisconsin's amazing fans. They chanted "Roooon Daayyynne" after each carry. They held up the towels. They shook the stadium that day. One fan even took off his clothes.

Alvarez has said he enjoyed proving people wrong and he often told his teams that there is nothing like doing something no one thinks you can do. That theme – doing the unexpected – appears again and again in these pages. Walk-ons become captains and all-conference players. Fans engage in the kind of spontaneity usually reserved for Hollywood. The magical occurrences that are part of college football lore at powerhouses like Ohio State, Alabama, Texas and USC? They now are part of Wisconsin tradition, too. And a 260-pound high school ball carrier from New Jersey – tabbed by most colleges as a fullback – goes to Wisconsin, becomes a tailback and runs for more yards than anyone else before him.

CHAPTER ONE
Setting the Wheels in Motion

As his Iowa Hawkeyes prepared for the final month of the 1995 season, head coach Hayden Fry considered the two Big Ten schools to which he had never lost during his 17-year tenure. One of those programs was Northwestern, which Iowa had been one-sidedly dismantling since the Wildcats' last win in the series in 1973. The Hawkeyes had won 21 consecutive games – 16 straight under Fry's direction – against Northwestern and had scored at least 45 points in nine of those contests. The other school Fry had mastered was Wisconsin.

The Badgers entered the 1995 season having lost 15 of their last 16 games against Iowa. (Fry was 13-0-1 against the Badgers during that stretch.) The only bright spot for Wisconsin in the series had come in 1984 when head coach Dave McClain's Hall of Fame Bowl-bound team tied Fry's 17th-ranked Hawkeyes, 10-10, in Iowa City. Aside from that, however, the Badgers had experienced nothing but frustration in meeting after meeting with Iowa since the first year of Jimmy Carter's presidency. And in years in which it seemed Wisconsin would have had a better-than-normal shot at knocking off their rivals to the southwest – 1993 and 1994, for example – the two schools did not play each other.

The 1995 campaign was, of course, a magical one for Northwestern. Head coach Gary Barnett's team, featuring stars like Darnell Autry, DeWayne Bates and Pat Fitzgerald, was focused on "Taking the Purple to Pasadena." On their way to the Big Ten title and a Rose Bowl appearance that season, the

Wildcats ended their stretch of futility against Iowa when Autry carried for 110 yards to help his fifth-ranked club to a 31-20 triumph in Evanston on November 11. It was the Hawkeyes' fourth consecutive defeat, and they were installed as seven-point underdogs heading into their game the following Saturday against the Badgers at Camp Randall Stadium in Madison.

Wisconsin's 1995 season had been an uneven one. The Badgers were routed, 43-7, in their season opener at home against 13th-ranked Colorado before picking up a tie at Stanford and back-to-back victories at home over SMU and at sixth-ranked Penn State. The win over the Nittany Lions on September 30 was one of the program's biggest under head coach Barry Alvarez and was unquestionably Wisconsin's most noteworthy victory that season. Penn State, coming off a 12-0 record in 1994, was the defending Big Ten and Rose Bowl champion and was riding a nation-leading 20-game winning streak. The Nittany Lions, who featured standout receivers Bobby Engram and Freddie Scott on an offense that was averaging nearly 50 points per game, had not lost at Beaver Stadium since October 16, 1993. But the Badgers, led by quarterback Darrel Bevell's incredibly efficient passing – he completed 18 of 22 aerials for 192 yards, two touchdowns and no interceptions – and a stellar defensive effort that included defensive tackle Jason Maniecki's memorable sack of Penn State quarterback Wally Richardson (he brought down Penn State guard and future Green Bay Packer Marco Rivera on the play, too) on the Nittany Lions' last drive, stunned the home crowd of 96,540 and a national television audience by winning 17-9. Alvarez thought at the time that his team would be alright as long as it continued to improve, but that did not happen.

Wisconsin followed the huge victory at State College with back-to-back losses at home against No. 4 Ohio State and at 11th-ranked Northwestern. The Badgers then sandwiched wins over Michigan State and Minnesota around a 38-27 loss at Purdue on November

4. Wisconsin was still fighting for a third straight bowl game appearance as its November 18 matchup with Iowa approached.

"Our kids really don't know much about Iowa ... (but) I do," Alvarez said the week of the game, referencing not only the fact the two programs had not met since 1992, but also that 25 current Badgers were not even alive the last time Wisconsin defeated Iowa. "Some of these guys have never played against them. They don't know anything about a rivalry with Iowa. They really don't. But we'll educate them. When was the last time a Wisconsin team beat Iowa? It was the mid-'70s. They've got to know that because they've got a chance to do something some other Wisconsin teams didn't get to do." Doing something others had not done – or that others thought unlikely or impossible – was a theme Alvarez often returned to with his teams during his 16 seasons as the head of the Badgers' program. The 1995 Badgers had shown that capability with the upset win at Penn State, but they had played inconsistently all season and were about to close the campaign on a sour note.

Wisconsin lost more starters (14) from its 1994 team than any other Big Ten school. The Badgers' 1995 schedule was rated as the most difficult in the nation by the *Seattle Times*. And more than a dozen players from the 1995 "two-deep" ended up in the National Football League. But the elements of Alvarez's best teams at Wisconsin – a dominating ground game, a tough defense and excellent special teams play – were not evident on a game-in, game-out basis in 1995. Carl McCullough, the team's starting tailback, would finish the season as just the third sophomore in school history to rush for 1,000 yards (1,038 to be exact), but he eclipsed the 100-yard mark just twice after the third game of the season and scored only three touchdowns. In the 40-year period from 1968-2008, only three Wisconsin teams averaged fewer than 140 rushing yards per game. Two of them were the 1990 and 1991 teams that combined to go 6-16 while Alvarez was turning the program around. The other was the 1995 club that averaged 128.9 yards per game and rushed for a league-worst 12 touchdowns.

On the other side of the ball, the Badgers allowed the second-most yards per game (394.7) of any Alvarez-era Wisconsin team. The "feast or famine" nature of the unit's performance was illustrated in its 170.6 yards-per-game run defense (third-worst of the Alvarez era): five opponents failed to rush for 100 yards that season, while six others surpassed the 200-yard mark. On special teams, aside from Aaron Stecker being the conference's No. 2 kick-off returner, the Badgers had no one ranked among the Big Ten's top nine punt returners; John Hall was ninth in the league in kick scoring; and Brian Alexander was 10th in the conference in punting average. It's important to understand some of these statistical points of reference. In contrast to what the Badgers had done the previous two seasons, as well as to what was to come, they paint a picture of a program in transition, one that was looking to regain its identity. Nothing drove that point home like the 1995 Iowa game.

Wisconsin fell behind, 24–7, by halftime that day and went on to drop a 33–20 decision to the Hawkeyes. The Badgers fought back and made a game of it in the second half, but the numbers told the story. Wisconsin rushed 20 times for minus 18 yards, while allowing Iowa's Sedrick Shaw to run wild, carrying the ball 41 times for 214 yards and three touchdowns. Shaw's effort gave him 280 rushing attempts for 1,304 yards, both Iowa records for a season. Bevell completed 35 of 51 passing attempts for 352 yards, but added four interceptions. His 35 completions (a school-record 13 went to tight end Matt Nyquist) were a UW record and his 352 yards were the fourth-most ever by a Badger quarterback. (Hidden behind Bevell's numbers, however, was this telling piece of information: at the time, the top six individual passing yardage efforts in Wisconsin history had come in losses.) Iowa had the ball more than 11 minutes longer than the Badgers. Fry had improved his record to 14-0-1 against Wisconsin, and his Hawkeyes had eliminated the Badgers from bowl contention.

This was not the Wisconsin football formula for success. The Badgers were supposed to grind their opponent down and impose their will with a punishing running game. The opponent should be forced to abandon its own ground game and throw more than it wanted to. Wisconsin was supposed to control the clock, win the turnover battle and execute on special teams. But none of that was happening, and Alvarez vowed after a dissatisfying, season-ending 3-3 tie at home with Illinois to "take our whole program, we'll dissect it, we'll go through it with a fine-tooth comb." He continued, "The thing that bothers me, the thing that concerns me the most and upsets me the most about the whole season is that we didn't get better after the Ohio State game. We've got to go back and take everything apart."

A dissection may have been in order, but in hindsight, the wheels had already been set in motion for Badger football to set the bar even higher than it had been in 1993 and, in doing so, take an entire athletic department along with it. For in the stadium on that cold, 34-degree day against Iowa in 1995 were at least a dozen players who would be key contributors to the program's championship teams of the late 1990s. Much of the remainder of the core of those clubs, in addition to some who would walk on, would soon sign national letters of intent to attend Wisconsin and play for the Badgers. One of the players in Camp Randall Stadium watching the Badgers fall to Iowa that day was also one who would soon sign with Wisconsin. His name was Ron Dayne.

CHAPTER TWO
Recruiting Ron Dayne

Bernie Wyatt came to Wisconsin as the recruiting coordinator and tight ends coach in 1991. Wyatt was born in Brooklyn, New York, and starred as a prep running back at Amityville High School where he earned All-American honors and broke many records set by NFL Hall of Fame running back Jim Brown. Wyatt went on to play football at Iowa and was the Hawkeyes' MVP in 1960. He later played in the Blue-Gray game and spent one season with the Pittsburgh Steelers. Wyatt was a successful high school coach before joining the coaching staff at his alma mater in 1974. He became Iowa's first full-time recruiting coordinator in 1979.

Early in his coaching career at Iowa, Wyatt developed a relationship with the late Ron Hopson, who had known the family of Ron Dayne's mother and had coached some of his uncles in high school. Hopson had become an assistant principal at Overbrook High School in Pine Hill, New Jersey, and was instrumental in guiding several young men to college football teams, including Leroy Smith, the 1991 Big Ten Defensive Player of the Year and a consensus All-American end for the Hawkeyes. Wyatt left Iowa in 1990 to join Alvarez's rebuilding effort at Wisconsin, but the Hopson-Wyatt relationship continued to yield recruits, including Lee DeRamus, Michael London and Keith Jackson – all of whom attended Edgewood Regional, where Hopson taught prior to working at Overbrook. Hopson had known Wyatt and Alvarez from their days as assistants at Iowa and he trusted them when they began recruiting Dayne.

"A lot of recruiting is knowing people and winning their trust," said Wyatt. "Ron Hopson really believed in the Wisconsin program and in Barry and myself, and he knew we would take care of the kid as far as guidance because he had worked with us earlier. He was on our side because we had earned his trust. He was the guy that actually turned me on to Ron Dayne."

Wyatt first saw Dayne in person not on the football field, but at a track meet where he was throwing the shot put and discus. Hopson had told Wyatt that Dayne was an exceptional athlete and that became abundantly clear to Wyatt as well.

"When I first saw him, I thought 'Wow!'" Wyatt said. "They're talking about him being a running back and I'd never seen a running back that big before. But Ron, for as big as he was, had pretty good quickness and that was the thing that led me to believe he could be a good tailback. He wasn't just a straight-line guy where if somebody got in his way he'd just run right over them. He could do that, too, but he could also make people miss him."

Brian White, then in his first year as running backs coach at Wisconsin, recalled Wyatt stopping by his office in Camp Randall Stadium one day to tell him about Dayne. "Coach Wyatt comes into my office and says, 'I've got a great tailback for you, Brian. He's 270 pounds.' I said 'Oh, yeah, I'd love to look at him, Bernie.' I'm thinking, 'a 270-pound tailback? I can't wait to see this.'"

White was stunned when he saw Dayne, in his dark navy and orange Overbrook Rams uniform, run over, around and through would-be tacklers.

"I watched the tape and thought, 'Holy cow, does he have some rare physical abilities!' Speed, change of direction and, obviously, the incredible power. That was my first introduction to him. I couldn't believe it."

Like Wyatt, White also had the chance to see Dayne at a track meet.

"I remember watching him at a high school track meet the spring of his senior year," White said. "I watched him throw the discus and to see that coordinated explosion of the balance, the power, the agility. I just said, 'This guy is really something else.'"

Wyatt showed Alvarez the tape of Dayne.

"When I saw Ron on tape, I saw two things," Alvarez said. "I saw him line up at fullback about two yards behind the quarterback and he'd go into the line, you'd see the line move, and maybe he'd come out the other end. But when you saw him at tailback – every once in a while they would line him up at tailback – he really had a patience about him, he could see things really well and I just said, 'He's a natural tailback. Even though he's 260-some pounds, he's a tailback.'"

Cecil Martin, then a redshirt freshman fullback for the Badgers, saw Dayne on tape, too.

"I remember walking through the football office one time and Coach Wyatt tells me he's got this running back in New Jersey who is 5-10, 265 pounds. I'm like, 'Get out of here!' But he put the tape of Ron Dayne in the VCR and I saw this big guy running up and down the field, running over people, running away from people. I said, 'This is unbelievable.'"

Dayne participated in football, track and wrestling in high school, and his accomplishments on the football field, as well as the track, were off the charts. Playing in the same backfield with his cousin Rob Reid Jr., who eventually played football at Tennessee-Chattanooga, Dayne rushed for close to 4,000 yards and 58 touchdowns in his football career, including 1,785 yards and 24 scores as a senior. His most notable performance that season was a 250-yard, four-touchdown effort against Edgewood Regional. The previous year, he carried for 1,566 yards and 27 touchdowns. He was a consensus high school All-American, appearing as the fullback on teams selected by *USA Today* and *Parade* magazine. Two recruiting publications tabbed him as the top fullback in the nation.

He was nearly as good in track and field. At the Golden West Invitational in Sacramento, California, on June 8, 1996, Dayne threw the discus 216 feet, 11 inches, at the time the third-longest discus throw in American high school history. He was named that meet's outstanding male athlete and earned the rare distinction of appearing in *Sports Illustrated*'s "Faces in the Crowd" feature in the September 16, 1996, edition. Just three days earlier, Dayne had smashed his own state discus record of 208 feet at the New Jersey State Interscholastic Athletic Association's "Meet of Champions" with a throw of 215 feet, 3 inches. Dayne, who also won the shot put (63 feet, 10 ¼ inches) at the 1996 NJSIAA meet, actually was concerned he had thrown the discus too far. "I was thinking, 'Oh man, I hope it doesn't go over the fence,'" Dayne told the *Newark Star-Ledger* that day, expressing concern that he wouldn't get a mark if he cleared the fence in right field of the baseball diamond. Dayne even provisionally qualified for the United States Olympic Trials. Amazingly, he had only been throwing the discus for a couple years, according to Hopson. Dayne said the shot put – he had a college-sized, 16-pound version – was something he "used to practice off our driveway, to throw into the yard."

But Dayne's future was on the football field and college recruiters were calling. Dayne's uncle, Rob Reid, with whom Dayne lived in high school after his parents' divorce and his mother's drug problems, remembers Maryland being the first school to contact his home. But Dayne had heard other area players, including DeRamus, rave about Wisconsin, and once Dayne visited Madison himself, he was sold. Because of his size, he was being projected by most coaching staffs as a college fullback, but he wanted the chance to carry the ball.

"Wisconsin and Michigan State were the only schools that wanted me to be a running back," Dayne recalled. "Once Coach (Alvarez) gave me that opportunity and I came and visited, it was a done deal."

The frenzy that developed around college football recruiting once the Internet and the 24-hour news cycle took hold had not quite materialized when Dayne was a high school senior, but there were media in Wisconsin who were covering recruiting and trying to keep tabs on Dayne's decision-making process. Reports at the time mentioned Ohio State, North Carolina State, Penn State, Notre Dame, Michigan, Clemson, Tennessee and others all being in the Dayne derby. The *Wisconsin State Journal* finally reported on November 23, 1995, that Dayne had visited Wisconsin, watched the Badgers' 33-20 loss to the Hawkeyes the previous weekend and committed to the UW after that.

Reid, Dayne's uncle, said,"Wisconsin was the school he always wanted to come to."

White recalls visiting with Dayne at that Iowa game.

"I remember being in the locker room with Ron (Dayne), Bernie (Wyatt) and Ron Hopson and telling him how obvious it was that he could play a significant role as a freshman," White said.

Alvarez recalls asking Dayne if he liked carrying the ball, and Dayne "nodded his head and grinned." The coach then told Dayne, "Well, I'll give you the damn ball as many times as you want it." But Alvarez gave Dayne something else, as well: a trustworthy father figure with whom the young man could form a solid relationship.

Dayne had come from a difficult family situation, and Hopson told Alvarez that Dayne needed someone to reach out to him.

"You could see there was a distance there," said Alvarez. "Ron was looking for someone to get close to, someone he could really trust. I remember he was kind of shy, but when he came in I went over to him and made a big fuss over him and gave him a big hug. And to this day, that's how we greet each other. Hopson said that over the years Ronnie and I had a very good bond. It started from right there because Hopson gave me some very good insight into the kid and how to deal with him, that he was looking to get close to a head coach. And that's what I tried to do."

Dayne had given the Badgers his verbal commitment, but at his uncle's urging made an additional campus visit a couple weeks later.

"I told Ronnie we needed to make a comparison and visit somewhere else," Reid said. "I almost forced him to go to Ohio State for a visit to at least make the comparison."

Reid and Dayne visited Ohio State the weekend of December 8, which also happened to be the weekend of the 1995 Heisman Trophy presentation.

"We went out to dinner with the Ohio State people," Reid said. "We're in this restaurant when they announce that their running back (Eddie George) won the Heisman Trophy and their people said 'See, that's why you need to come to Ohio State. You'll win the Heisman!' But Ronnie was really sold on Wisconsin. Coach Alvarez and Coach Wyatt were great. When we were going through the recruiting process, Bernie was no-pressure, really easy to talk to, told us what to expect and how he would really watch out for Ron while he was in Wisconsin. I can't say enough about Bernie. Wisconsin was just a place that was tailor-made for Ron."

CHAPTER THREE
On to Wisconsin

The success of a major college football program depends upon more than just a good coaching staff and a group of talented athletes. Numerous athletic department employees, known at the University of Wisconsin as support staff, help teams run smoothly. Athletic trainers, strength and conditioning coaches, personnel overseeing academics, nutritionists, equipment managers, video staff and media relations personnel are all key to a team functioning well. There are also others – professors, roommates, girlfriends, friends from back home – outside the athletic department who can play significant roles in the lives of college football players. In addition to his future teammates and coaches, Ron Dayne would, during the summer of 1996, meet a number of people who would play extraordinarily important roles in his life in the coming years.

John Dettmann came to Wisconsin as a strength and conditioning coach in 1990 – the same year Barry Alvarez took over as head coach – and was named director of his department two years later. Dettmann worked primarily with the football team. He had been an honorable mention All-American wide receiver, team MVP and Athlete of the Year at the University of Wisconsin-Oshkosh, where he earned a degree in corporate fitness. He signed a free agent contract with the Green Bay Packers in 1982 before entering the private sector until his arrival in Madison. In his role, Dettmann saw the Badger football players as much, if not more, than their position coaches, so he naturally got an early glimpse once Dayne and his teammates arrived for conditioning drills in the summer of 1996.

"What I remember was – for a player his size – his burst, his power and his quickness," Dettmann said. "Ron had great hip and leg strength, great feet. He could accelerate and, for a kid that size, that was the surprising piece of it. The reality of it was that the things people saw on the field, we'd see too ... the quickness, the feet, his reaction. I remember him being pretty special for a kid his size. His conditioning level wasn't quite where it would need to be by the time we got to camp; he couldn't sustain, but he could show you flashes of the ability he had."

One of the other heavily recruited players that joined Dayne at Wisconsin that summer was quarterback Scott Kavanagh. Kavanagh was a prep All-American at Naperville North High School in Illinois, where he threw for 3,008 yards and 33 touchdowns during his career. He led his team to the state title game as a junior and already knew something about the college game because his brother, Brian, was a quarterback at Kansas State. Kavanagh and Dayne were among 13 newcomers on scholarship who had moved to Madison for summer conditioning, an unusually high number in those days.

"Normally we don't have any or you might have a handful that are in the Summer Collegiate Experience," Alvarez said. "Those kids have wound up being pretty close friends and all wanted to come here and live together during the summer."

The close relationships developed by the players who came into the Wisconsin football program in the mid-1990s would remain a characteristic of the Badgers' Big Ten title teams of 1998 and 1999.

Dettmann wasn't the only one at summer conditioning drills who could see Dayne's potential. In fact, Cecil Martin, a fullback and sophomore-to-be, had perceived it, albeit incorrectly, back on Dayne's recruiting visit at the Iowa game the previous fall.

"I remember thinking to myself that there was probably no way he's going to end up playing running back here; he's probably going to end up playing fullback and I'm going to end up backing him up or something," Martin said in an obvious reference to Dayne's size.

But Martin became a believer once he saw the freshman from New Jersey work out that summer.

"We ran 10-yard dashes and we ran shuttles," he said. "We had Carl McCullough, who had just come off a 1,000-yard season as a sophomore. We had Aaron Stecker, who was short and quick and an all-around great athlete. And Ron Dayne ran a faster 10 and a faster shuttle than both of them. That's when I knew there was something special here. There was nothing about him when he walked onto the field that told you he could do that, but the watch doesn't lie."

Another of the first-year Badgers was Donnel Thompson, who like everyone else recognized Dayne's freakish athletic ability, but thought the running back looked more suited to playing on the line of scrimmage.

"I saw this big guy who looked like he carried the weight of a small defensive lineman, but a little too short," Thompson said. "I was trying to figure out what position he played. Then I saw him go through the ladders. You can really work on your foot speed. Once I saw him go through the ladders, I realized he had to be some type of skill position because I had never seen anybody's feet – with that type of size – move that quickly."

Thompson, a walk-on from Madison, not only became close friends with Dayne but also made a life-changing introduction to his new teammate from the East Coast. Donnel Thompson and his brother, Bryson, who would also play for the Badgers, grew up on Rowley Avenue, just off Regent Street, a few blocks from Camp Randall Stadium. When Donnel was about six years old, he and Bryson would hold parking signs on Badger football game days, trying to steer cars in the direction of their house where their father, Curtis, would negotiate a price. A few years later, Donnel was earning his own keep at Badger football games.

"It was working for the W Club," Donnel recalled. "In fact, my dad played (tight end) for the Madison Mustangs and had a great career and went on to the pro's. His quarterback with the Mustangs was Terry Murawski, executive director of the national W Club. My dad told him I was interested in a job and Terry told him to send me over. So, because of my dad's old football connections, I was able to start selling Cokes over at the University of Wisconsin. I was one of the top sellers, probably because I was one of the biggest kids. I did that from the time I was 12 or 13 until I was 17."

Donnel Thompson was a standout linebacker playing for his father at Madison West High School. He was an all-conference player as a junior and was "receiving letters from most Big Ten schools and a lot of schools in the Midwest." That was until he broke his right arm during the third game of his senior year.

"Surprise, surprise," Donnel said. "A lot of the schools were no longer interested in the short linebacker (he was 6-0, 215) with the broken arm. A lot of the calls and letters stopped coming."

But Wisconsin offered Donnel the chance to walk-on to the program as a freshman, and he jumped at the opportunity. He ended up earning a scholarship, serving as captain of two Big Ten championship teams (1998 and 1999) and becoming a tremendous leader and integral part of the Ron Dayne-era teams at Wisconsin. Donnel played a season with the Pittsburgh Steelers and three with the Indianapolis Colts before a knee injury ended his career.

One of Donnel Thompson's high school friends was Alia Lester, who had moved with her parents – before they divorced – to Madison from Great Lakes Naval Base in Illinois in 1990.

Lester hung out with Donnel and Bryson Thompson, often playing football with them near Blessed Sacrament Parish on a patch of land they called "the triangle." They attended West High School together, and Donnel and Alia were preparing for their freshman year at Wisconsin when her birthday rolled around on July 15.

Lester planned a barbeque and, knowing Donnel was going to become a part of the Wisconsin football program, told her friend to feel free to bring a few of his future teammates over to her house for the birthday party. Lester and her mother, who was outside tending to the grill, were more than a little surprised when what looked like the entire Badger depth chart showed up. Thompson later confessed to Lester that he basically had gone into the Badgers' locker room and asked, "Who wants free food?" Lester's wide-eyed mother headed across the street to buy more meat.

"It was definitely scary for my mom," Alia said. "She was looking at Gibby (6-foot-7, 378-pound offensive lineman Aaron Gibson) and Cecil (Martin) and the others and thinking they needed food. Much more of it!"

One of the hungry Badgers was Dayne but, according to Lester, the two didn't hit it off at first. "It was not an immediate love-at-first-sight scenario," Alia recalls. "He thought I was stuck up and I thought he looked mean." Dayne, however, later asked Donnel Thompson about Lester, and Thompson — without Lester's knowledge — gave Dayne her phone number. Lester arranged to meet Dayne at the Helen C. White Library on campus where they got a chance to talk. They started dating in the fall of 1996.

"I tell him all the time when we first met, he would just talk," Lester said of Dayne. "People cannot believe that Ron would just talk. He'd tell me stories, stories about his family. He spent like a month of talking and then he ran out of things to say and that's been it! He told me everything about his family and I felt really comfortable because I also grew up in a situation where my dad was gone."

Years later, Martin would observe, "I think it wasn't necessarily a choice as much as it was those two came together for each other and really, probably, filled a space for each other."

Both Dayne and Lester had experienced the adversity and emotional pain that comes with the breakup of a family and the similarities in their backgrounds, Lester recalled, helped the pair to "fight to not be like that."

Yet another key person Dayne met prior to the start of his freshman season at Wisconsin was Steve Malchow, then the director of the UW men's sports information office and the primary publicity and media relations contact for the Badger football program. Malchow grew up in Sioux City, Iowa, the son of a sports writer (his father, Ron, worked at the *Sioux City Journal*), and went on to attend the University of Iowa where he earned degrees in marketing and management information systems, with a minor in journalism and mass communications. While at Iowa, Malchow worked as an undergraduate student assistant in the school's sports information office. He was eventually hired as a full-time assistant, working closely with the Hawkeyes' men's basketball team from 1985-89.

The Wisconsin sports information office was in transition as Barry Alvarez was taking over as head coach of the football team. The late Jim Mott, the men's sports information director from 1966-90, was retiring and that opened the door for Malchow, who had known Alvarez when the two were working at Iowa. Malchow arrived in Madison in the summer of 1990 and was a first-hand witness to the rebuilding of UW athletics as a whole, and the football program in particular. He was experienced and hard-working and he took his job seriously – all traits that would prove beneficial as he began working with the rather quiet and reserved Dayne.

It is probably not accurate to say there was a definite level of expectation for Dayne on the part of Badger fans and the media that covered the Badgers' 1996 training camp. Certainly there had been coverage of Dayne's recruitment and signing, along with the periodic reports of his high school exploits (especially in track and field). But few Wisconsin football fans or media had seen Dayne on tape. There was no You Tube or Facebook or Twitter. The internet, as we now know it, was in its infancy. The instant communication that is so much a part of the world today and contributes so much to the immediate shaping of our views and opinions was not as prevalent in those days. Rather than expectation, there was a clear degree of curiosity and anticipation about Dayne.

Mike Lucas, the longtime *Capital Times* columnist and radio color analyst for Badger sports, wrote a story in early June of 1996 that mentioned Dayne's ability to dunk a basketball and discussed his phenomenal accomplishments in the discus. Even UW track and field coach Ed Nuttycombe weighed in, telling Lucas, "Ron Dayne is an extraordinary athlete." Later that summer, at the Big Ten Football Media Days in Chicago, Alvarez was quizzed by the assembled group of reporters about a number of issues and Dayne, of course, was one of them. About his own expectations for Dayne to contribute as a freshman, Alvarez said, "It's hard for me to say right now. I really believe he's a special athlete, but a lot will depend on how soon he picks things up, how he makes that adjustment, how he takes to college football and learns the system. The good thing is, we're not counting on him. He can run and he's got quickness. He weighs 267 and has been there all summer. I think he's in pretty good shape. That's a pretty big body coming at you and I'd like for him to be able to play. But I'm not going to get optimistic till I see him on the field and see where he is."

CHAPTER FOUR
The Freshman Phenom

As freshman training camp opened on August 14, 1996, one of the first drills Brian White conducted with his stable of rookie runners practically cost the second-year Badger running backs coach his life. White was simulating a linebacker running straight at the running back, whose job it was to cut opposite the direction in which White leaned and head up field with the ball. The drill was designed to evaluate the running back's lateral movement and ability to quickly move north or south with the ball. Dayne almost hit White head-on.

"I leaned to the left and (Dayne) cut to (that same side) and it just flashed in front of my face, 'I'm going to get killed by this 270-pound guy who was running way too fast for me to be able to control myself,'" White recalls. "But he was agile enough to be able to make the wrong cut and then make another cut in an instant and get the ball to the other side. I looked over to the sideline and Barry just winked at me."

It was clear from the start that Dayne could do things that others, particularly players his size, could not. Alvarez had acknowledged just prior to the start of training camp that he was "anxious to see that one cat with the ball." Dayne had been tabbed by *Sports Illustrated* as the No. 5 freshman to watch in college football in 1996. He was even going to be wearing No. 33, the number he wore in high school, the same digits Alvarez wore as a linebacker at Nebraska in the mid-1960s and the same number donned by running back Brent Moss, the Badgers' 1993 Big

Ten and Rose Bowl MVP. But it was not as simple as handing the rookie the starting job.

"Looking back on it now, I give Barry Alvarez a lot of credit because he eased (Dayne) in," said Andy Baggot, who was covering the team for the *Wisconsin State Journal* at the time. "He did so with a gesture of respect to the guy in front of him. Carl McCullough ran for 1,000 yards the previous year. He was as highly touted coming out of high school as Ron Dayne was coming out of high school. It was a matter of 'you've got to earn your way in, you've got to show us.' I remember talking to Brian White at the time and he told me Ron Dayne was no different than anyone else. 'He's got to hit his landmarks just like everyone else. He's got to learn how to pick up blitzers. He's got to learn all these things. Until we feel comfortable that he can do all these things, we're not going to put him in there just to put him in there and let him start.' So, I think in their minds, he had to show [the coaches] that he's earned it."

In addition to McCullough and Dayne, the Badgers' running backs corps late in the summer of 1996 included redshirt sophomore Aaron Stecker, who rushed for 334 yards in 1995 and came to fall camp as the No. 2 back behind McCullough; redshirt freshmen Charles Williams and Jean Jourdain; and true freshman Eddie Faulkner, Dayne's roommate who, with his shiftiness and cutback abilities, was drawing comparisons to a young version of former Badger star Terrell Fletcher. McCullough could most identify with the buzz surrounding Dayne. Like Dayne, he had been a consensus high school All-American, appearing on teams compiled by *USA Today* and *Parade* magazine. He had rushed for almost 2,000 yards as a high school senior at Cretin Derham Hall in St. Paul, Minnesota, in 1992 and came to Wisconsin in 1993 with a spotlight already on him despite the fact the Badger backfield included both Moss, the eventual Big Ten MVP, as well as Fletcher. McCullough saw the roles reversed when the Badgers met with local and statewide reporters at the team's media day session at

Camp Randall Stadium on August 18.

Alvarez had approached Malchow earlier in the week and asked him to talk with mammoth offensive lineman Aaron Gibson and Dayne about how media day worked and what the two could expect. The pair had yet to step on the field for the Badgers – Gibson was ineligible in 1995 – but they were the focus of much attention, and Alvarez wanted Malchow to prepare them for what can be an overwhelming experience for a young person who has not been through it before. It was the first time Malchow had met Dayne.

"I remember talking to 'Gibby' and he was really outgoing, fun-loving, laughed a lot and we had a good exchange," Malchow recalled. "My first meeting with Ron, I won't forget it. We were sitting on the steps there (at the Holy Name Seminary where the Badgers trained in those days) and I spoke to him for about 10 minutes about what media day was going to entail. He never said a word. He never responded to me at all. He nodded at me a couple times and kind of smiled. I remember getting done with the session and Coach Alvarez asked me at dinner that night if I'd had the chance to talk to the two freshmen. I said I had talked to one of them, but the other one just listened to me. He obviously knew which one was the quiet one. [Alvarez] asked me if I thought Ron would get through media day, and I said, 'I don't know, Coach. I got no read out of him. He was attentive, but he gave me no feedback whatsoever. It'll be interesting on media day.'"

Dayne got through media day, but Malchow and the reporters with whom he was responsible for working found out that the freshman from New Jersey was not one to waste his words. He was polite, to be sure, but he just did not have much to say, particularly about himself. Baggot gleaned a few nuggets from Dayne – the running back said he never really lifted weights in high school – but the headline in the *Wisconsin State Journal* the next day pretty well summarized Dayne's first media day appearance: "UW's Dayne lets talent do talking: Hyped freshman doesn't reveal much to media."

Dayne's teammates, however, were less reserved.

"I have never seen a mass that big move with that much quickness and that much strength," said right guard and fifth-year senior Cayetano Castro.

Years later another offensive lineman, then a redshirt freshman, would recall Dayne's freshman fall camp performance.

"He had some flashes of brilliance in camp that would make people look twice at him and the way he'd move," said Chris McIntosh, who would start at left tackle for Dayne's entire collegiate career. "When Barry would have a live scrimmage and really turn up the tempo, that was when Ron would really lower his shoulder and you'd get a glimpse of what he became famous for down the road."

The 1996 Badgers, who were scheduled to open the season on September 7 with a home game against Eastern Michigan, were looking to rebound from their 4-5-2 record of a year earlier, and they would try to do that with an experienced team that featured eight starters on each side of the ball, as well as the return of senior John Hall, who would handle just about all the kicking and punting duties. Critical, of course, to the Wisconsin offense was the line and, unlike the previous season, the Badgers had veterans up front. Senior right tackle Jerry Wunsch and senior left guard Jamie Vanderveldt were both honorable mention All-Big Ten picks in 1995. The duo entered 1996 with a combined 40 starts between them. Castro had started 11 times at left tackle the year before, but was moved to right guard for his final campaign. Senior Derek Engler was slated to take over at center and McIntosh took up permanent residence at left tackle.

Quarterback Darrell Bevell, who finished his college career in 1995 as the school's winningest signal-caller and who helped lead the Badgers to the 1993 Big Ten title, was being replaced by sophomore Mike Samuel. Samuel, a native of Philadelphia, had thrown just 31 passes as a Badger, but it would be Samuel's mental and physical toughness, his running ability and his leadership skills that would, for the next three years, key the Badgers. And when Samuel did throw the ball, he had solid wide receivers Tony Simmons and Donald Hayes as targets.

Sophomore Cecil Martin had emerged as a freshman in 1995 and would end up starting the final three seasons of his career at fullback.

The focal point of the Badgers' defense in 1996 was senior rush end Tarek Saleh, who left Wisconsin as the school's career leader in tackles for loss and quarterback sacks. Saleh was joined by defensive veterans like senior linebackers Pete Monty (the school's all-time leading tackler) and Daryl Carter, and defensive backs Kevin Huntley, Jason Suttle and Cyrill Weems.

A number of freshmen and first-year starters – Samuel, McIntosh, Bob Adamov, Tom Burke, Chris Ghidorzi, Donnel Thompson, Bobby Myers, Tim Rosga, Mike Schneck, Chris Janek, Scott Kavanagh and Ross Kolodziej – saw action in 1996, helping to lay the groundwork for the back-to-back Big Ten championship teams of the late 1990s. A player who was neither a freshman nor a first-year starter in 1996 – huge sophomore Aaron Gibson – would also see action that season and help forge the program's identity of that era.

The week of the 1996 opener against Eastern Michigan, the Badgers received votes but were outside the preseason top-25 polls. Dayne was listed as the No. 3 tailback on the depth chart the Badgers released prior to the game. Alvarez publicly stated that McCullough would start and that Stecker would be the next man in.

"I don't have a set number (of repetitions) for each of them," Alvarez said before the game. "We'll start with Carl. Aaron will be the next one in line. If either one of them is real hot, they'll just keep going. Ron Dayne will play in the first half, but I don't know who's going to get the most carries. We'll just see who looks sharpest."

Eastern Michigan, a 24-point underdog heading into the nationally-televised (ESPN2) contest in Madison, had opened its own season a week earlier with a 28-24 loss to Temple. The Eagles featured future NFL quarterback Charlie Batch, who threw for more than 3,100 yards in 1995, but they were not expected to put up much of a fight against the veteran Badgers. Wisconsin forced Eastern Michigan to punt on its opening drive, and the Badgers took over at their own 48-yard line. Samuel immediately directed the Badgers to their first touchdown of the season. Making his debut as the starting quarterback, Samuel rushed for 11 yards and passed for 11 yards on the scoring drive, while McCullough picked up his longest run of the day (21 yards) and punctuated the drive with a 4-yard touchdown run around the right side for a 7-0 lead. But the Wisconsin offense was plagued by three quarterback sacks and three penalties in the first half and went to the locker room at halftime with that same 7-0 advantage. UW opened the second half with a 48-yard scoring drive and added a field goal by Hall later in the third quarter for a 17-0 lead heading into the final frame.

Wisconsin had assumed possession of the ball at its own 26 after the Eagles missed a field goal attempt with 14:52 remaining in the fourth quarter. A 32-yard gain on a third-down reverse by receiver Ahmad Merritt took the Badgers to the Eagles' 42 and that is where the Ron Dayne era at Wisconsin officially began. McCullough left the game after the Merritt run and Dayne came in to "a collective murmur of anticipation in the crowd of 74,729."

On his first carry as a Badger, Dayne took a handoff from Samuel, got a nice block from Martin and rumbled up the middle for six yards. In a scenario that would be repeated time and time again in games to come, Dayne carried the ball on five consecutive plays, among those a 23-yarder over left tackle during which

McIntosh leveled his man, as the bruising rookie runner broke three tackles and dragged the last one four yards to the Eagles' 6-yard line. Two plays later Dayne followed left guard Jamie Vanderveldt and backup fullback Branden Cantrell around the left side and into the end zone from two yards out for the first of his 71 career touchdowns. Dayne punctuated the run with the high-stepping stomp that would become a trademark of his touchdown carries. The player tabbed by a *Milwaukee Journal Sentinel* columnist earlier that day as "the biggest curiosity to ever hit UW football" was a curiosity no longer.

Dayne rushed for 53 yards and the one touchdown on eight carries in his collegiate debut and did nothing to quell the growing sense among fans and media that it would just be a matter of time before he was assuming an increased, if not starting, role for the Badgers. Though Dayne carried only eight times and scored a touchdown that had little effect on the game's outcome, the main photo on page one of the *Wisconsin State Journal* sports section the next day featured Dayne.

"Everyone wanted to see him play," the coach said after his team's tougher-than-expected 24-3 win. "Quite frankly, I wanted to see him play."

But media were already questioning why Alvarez had waited until the fourth quarter to insert Dayne into the game and were even suggesting the Badgers live with the inevitable "rookie mistakes" as Dayne learned the offense because he was simply too talented to keep off the field. Alvarez, however, wisely balanced his postgame comments about Dayne, saying, "It's always nice to come in when the other team is behind and worn down a little bit. But it was good to get him his first action and I thought he did very well." Alvarez acknowledged Dayne's fine debut, but was also careful not to make too much of it. McCullough had rushed for 107 yards and a touchdown and Stecker had added another 56 yards rushing and receiving. They had done nothing to warrant a demotion.

One of the first players to greet Dayne with an enthusiastic bear hug after his touchdown was McCullough, who actually met the freshman on the UW sideline at the 20-yard line.

"That made me feel good because he's treated me like a brother, him and Steck and all the fullbacks," Dayne told the media after the game.

It was a sign of the relationship Dayne had developed with the other running backs.

"I think it's really critical to point out the role Carl McCullough and Aaron Stecker had in Ron's development," said Brian White. "It was a very healthy atmosphere. They really did a great job of nurturing him and helping him along and really mentored him extremely well. As competitive a situation as it was, it was also extremely healthy."

Martin recalled something similar when he thought about how McCullough handled Dayne's success and increasing popularity.

"I remember Carl jumping up and down and getting fired up about things the offense was doing in the running game when Ron did something really good," the sophomore fullback said. "He wasn't just standing there looking upset that success was happening. He was actually congratulating him."

One reporter asked McCullough after the Eastern Michigan game if he felt slighted by the reaction Dayne got from the crowd when he took the field.

"Hey, that's a big cat coming in," McCullough said. "He was a great player in high school coming in for us. Of course they're going to be excited to watch him play."

Wisconsin traveled to UNLV the next weekend and figured to run all over Coach Jeff Horton's Rebels, whose rushing defense was ranked 106th nationally. The Badgers met expectations but, again, Dayne did not see much playing time until the fourth quarter.

"I can remember putting him in the game early (it was about midway through the second quarter) and (offensive coordinator) Brad Childress saying, 'What are you doing?'" Alvarez remembered. "I said that I wanted to see [Dayne] in the game early when the bullets were flying. [Childress] didn't like that because we really hadn't talked about it, but sometimes, as a coach, I did things on a hunch."

Dayne ended up with just the one second-quarter carry for four yards until he returned to action very late in the third quarter with the Badgers in command, 38-17. Wisconsin took over on its own 20 after a UNLV field goal with 16 seconds left in the third stanza. Dayne carried for 15 yards on the first play and totaled 45 of UW's 80 yards on the drive, including a 1-yard scoring run. He finished the contest with 90 yards and one touchdown on just 13 carries. But Stecker had stolen the show that night by gaining 135 yards and a pair of touchdowns on only 12 attempts. In addition, he caught a pass for seven yards and contributed a 33-yard kickoff return. McCullough added 71 yards on 14 carries. Wisconsin won the game, 52-17, in front of an estimated 30,000 Badger fans who were among the crowd of 40,091 that made it the "largest gathering for a team sporting event in Nevada history."

Through the first two games of his career, Dayne had essentially been brought along slowly and had done what was asked of him. He had played late and performed well in two games against weak opponents who were already worn down by the time he got in. He certainly had done enough to hold the interest and capture the imagination of both media and fans. But he had not accomplished anything against a good defense or at a point in a game where it really meant something. That would come in week 3.

Second-year Stanford coach Tyrone Willingham, named the 1995 Pac-10 Coach of the Year after leading the Cardinal to a 7-4-1 record (after the program was 3-7-1 in 1994), brought a legitimate, tough defense to Camp Randall Stadium on September 21 for the Badgers' final non-conference game before the start of the Big Ten season. The Cardinal was allowing just 118 rushing yards and 9.5 points per game after its first two contests, and Willingham would admit after the game that his team's goal on defense was to stop the Badgers' running game. To a large degree, they did just that.

The game was a defensive slugfest. Wisconsin went three and out on its first three possessions and got very little going offensively until Samuel capped a 61-yard scoring drive with a 22-yard touchdown strike to Donald Hayes midway through the second quarter. In the meantime, the Badgers were shutting down Stanford as well. Wisconsin went to halftime with just two net rushing yards (including 22 for McCullough and minus one for Stecker), while the Cardinal had accumulated just 107 total net yards. The one bright spot for Wisconsin was Samuel, who completed 14 of 19 passes for 164 yards. The teams combined for five turnovers in a bizarre but scoreless third quarter, leaving the Badgers clinging to their 7-0 lead with 15 minutes left in regulation.

Dayne had not carried the ball to that point, but that changed when the Badgers took over at the Stanford 49 with 11:14 left to play. He was stopped for a 1-yard loss on his first attempt, but later in the drive ripped off runs of 13 and six yards that helped bring the Badgers to the Stanford 3-yard line. The drive, however, was wiped out when Samuel threw an interception in the end zone. Dayne hadn't yet been given a chance to make a real statement on the field, but the moment was at hand.

Wisconsin's defense forced a Stanford punt on the ensuing possession, and the Badgers took over on their own 45 with 6:27 remaining. The Cardinal had allowed the Badgers a mere 39 net rushing yards up to that point in the game. Then Dayne took over. He picked up 14 yards to open the drive and added a 17-yard gain four plays later. He carried the ball on eight consecutive plays, accumulating 54 yards and dragging the Badgers to the Stanford 1-yard line, where Samuel scored on a quarterback sneak to ice the game. Dayne sliced through a stingy defense with a game still in the balance. The Badgers went on to win 14-0, improving their record to 3-0. Dayne was UW's leading rusher that day (12 carries, 75 yards) despite the fact he didn't carry the ball until the fourth quarter. McCullough and Stecker had combined for 47 net yards on 18 carries in three quarters of work.

"I really liked what I saw from Ron," Alvarez said after the game. "He came in with fresh legs and made things happen, and it's not because he's 260 pounds. He makes quick cuts and he's always moving forward. There's a place for Ron, and probably much sooner than what we've seen."

That was music to the ears of Wisconsin fans, not to mention Dayne himself. The drumbeat for increased playing time for Dayne had grown louder by the week. Fans wanted to see more of him and the topic had become a focal point of local media coverage. Dayne had come to Wisconsin expecting to play and carry the ball, but he had been relegated to seeing action almost exclusively in the second half of the first three games. It was during this period of time that he briefly wondered whether he had made the right college choice. He actually called his mother and Ron Hopson and told them he was thinking he wanted to transfer to Michigan State because that was one of the schools that had told him he could play tailback. Brenda Reid preached patience.

"I said 'you've got to give them a chance,'" Brenda recalled. "I told him that once they saw what he could do, they would put him in there."

The issue would be put to rest once and for all very soon. If there was any remaining doubt about what Dayne could do after his performance against Stanford, he erased it for good the following week with a coming-of-age showing against one of the best teams in the nation: No. 3-ranked Penn State. The Badgers had never lost in three previous tries against Penn State, including the notable victory at State College in 1995. ABC was in Madison to televise the game to its split-national audience, and Camp Randall Stadium was drenched in sunshine, with the game-time temperature at 57 degrees. It was a classic early fall afternoon in Madison.

Alvarez had been less-than-forthcoming with the media during the week about how much Dayne would play, but it seemed clear the freshman would have ample opportunity to prove himself against a team that had shut out its last two opponents and ranked ninth nationally in total defense. However, the official depth chart remained the same, with McCullough listed as the starter, Stecker behind him and Dayne at No. 3.

"I'm sure we'll get him in the game much sooner," Alvarez said. "That's something that we'll decide this week how we're going to rotate them through."

Wisconsin opened the game with a 15-play, 50-yard drive that consumed 5:41 and ended with John Hall's 47-yard field goal that gave the Badgers a 3-0 lead. Penn State returned the favor on its ensuing possession, tying the game with a Brett Conway field goal from 33 yards out. That left the Badgers to start their next possession on their own 20 after Conway's kickoff went out of the back of the end zone for a touchback.

Dayne carried for just one yard on the first play of the drive, and three plays later Hall was punting. But it was the earliest Dayne had appeared in a game, a clear signal that he had indeed earned more playing time in the eyes of the Wisconsin coaches. Mark Jones, the play-by-play announcer for ABC, commented as Dayne was returning to the huddle after his run that the freshman had "quickly become the people's choice here in Madison."

Penn State responded with a pair of Curtis Enis touchdown runs and moved out to a 17-3 lead midway through the second quarter when Dayne came back into the game. The UW offense had sputtered since its opening scoring drive, but it was about to get a jolt. The Badgers took over at their own 35 with 10:18 left in the second quarter and put their ensuing drive on Dayne's back. He carried 11 times on the 14-play, 65-yard scoring march and even caught a 5-yard pass for good measure. It was classic Alvarez-style football and ended with Dayne dragging Penn State linebacker Aaron Collins into the end zone on a 6-yard run. Collins initially hit Dayne at the 3 on the play, but bounced off him and held on as Dayne fell forward across the goal line. It was another chapter in the developing story of Dayne's emergence, but there was more to come.

Penn State had gone ahead, 20-10, when Wisconsin took over at its own 14-yard line with 1:50 left in the third quarter. Dayne had played some since the long scoring drive, but Stecker and McCullough had been mixed in as well. Samuel hit Hayes on a 2-yard pass to set up second and eight. On the next play, Samuel handed to Dayne who got a key block from Castro and sprinted 50 yards for the longest run of his brief career. It took defensive back Shawn Lee to chase him down. The drive stalled, however, when Stecker fumbled after catching a pass.

The Wisconsin defense forced Penn State to turn the ball over on downs on its next possession, and the Badgers started on their own 30 with 11:29 left to play in regulation. Samuel completed four passes, ran once himself and left the rest to Dayne. On first and 10 from the Penn State 12, Dayne made one of the most memorable runs of his entire career. He took the ball from Samuel and carried around left end. Martin blocked safety Kim Herring, who had come up for run support. That left Dayne to contend with Collins, Lee and cornerback Mark Tate all by himself. Tate hit Dayne at the 7-yard line, but bounced off him. Collins then had Dayne fully in his grasp at the 5-yard line, but Dayne kept his legs moving and spun away from the same Penn

State linebacker he had carried into the end zone on his first touchdown. Lee made a last-ditch effort at the 2, but Dayne was already crossing the goal line. Years later Matt Lepay, the longtime radio play-by-play voice for the Badgers, would call it a "ridiculously physical, Earl Campbell-esque touchdown run" and that colorful description, referencing the legendary University of Texas and Houston Oiler running back, was right on the mark.

Wisconsin eventually tied the game at 20-20, but Conway put the Nittany Lions back ahead, 23-20, with a 25-yard field goal with 1:23 left. The Badgers gave Hall a shot to send the game to overtime, but his 58-yard attempt was a few feet wide to the left as time expired. Wisconsin had fallen short in its upset bid, but it had found its tailback of the future. He had certainly made believers of the Nittany Lions.

"We were just trying to hang in there, hang in there and stay composed under the pressure," Collins said after the game. "This is a great confidence-booster for us because they really put us to the test. That No. 33. He's big, he's tough and he can run. He's like 'Ironhead' Heyward." The late Heyward, a running back from New Jersey who became an All-American at the University of Pittsburgh in 1987 and an 11-year NFL veteran, had physical measurements similar to Dayne.

Dayne rushed for 129 yards and two touchdowns on 24 carries against Penn State. He became the third Badger – joining McCullough and Stecker – to rush for 100 yards in a game that season, but he was the only one of the three who would do it again in 1996. Dayne moved to the top of the depth chart following the Penn State game and remained there for the rest of his career. In rewarding Dayne, Alvarez pointed out that it wasn't just the freshman's long runs that were impressive.

"I said at the press conference that I thought his best runs were the third-and-ones," Alvarez told the Madison media two days after the loss to the Nittany Lions. "There were people unblocked at the point of attack, where contact was made behind the line of scrimmage – where he still gets us the first down. Normally, you're going to have to line up and punt the ball. But he's hard to bring down in that situation because he's so hard to get a hold of."

Wisconsin had a bye week before it had to travel to Columbus to meet No. 2-ranked Ohio State and that gave the Badgers time to tinker with their offensive line. The already-huge group was the biggest unit in the nation, averaging nearly 6-6, 310 pounds, but Alvarez and his staff decided to insert the 6-7, 378-pound Gibson. Gibson played tight end in the Badgers' "jumbo" formation against the Buckeyes and, at other times, McIntosh moved to the right side of the line with Wunsch. The adjustments helped keep Ohio State off balance, particularly in the first half. The Badgers led 7-3 at halftime and 14-10 after Kevin Huntley's 36-yard fumble recovery for a touchdown with 13:09 left in the fourth quarter. But the Buckeyes' Dimitrious Stanley caught a 48-yard touchdown pass from Joe Germaine with 8:51 remaining and Ohio State staved off the upset bid.

Dayne got his first start but, in reality, he and McCullough rotated through most of the game. McCullough led all rushers that day with 81 yards on 18 carries, while Dayne ended up with 65 yards on 21 carries. The Buckeyes had just hammered Penn State, 38-7, a week earlier and brought the nation's No. 6 defense into the game with the Badgers. In addition, Ohio State was averaging 52 points and 547 yards per game on offense, so Wisconsin acquitted itself well, but was forced to accept another near miss against a high-quality opponent. As painful as the losses to Penn State and Ohio State were, however, they would pale in comparison to what was to come next. Dayne was about to get his first taste of controversy as a college football player.

Wisconsin returned to Madison for its Homecoming contest against 14th-ranked and once-beaten Northwestern on October

19. ESPN was in the house to televise the game nationally and four different bowl games had scouts in attendance. The Badgers were looking to shake off their two previous losses, and head coach Gary Barnett's Wildcats, still riding the surprising wave of success that had begun a year earlier, were looking to move to 4-0 in conference play and keep their hopes of a second straight Big Ten title alive. It was a pivotal game for both teams.

Much like they had against the Nittany Lions and Buckeyes, the Badgers stood toe-to-toe with Northwestern on that cloudless, 52-degree day. A bad snap by Paul Janus that sailed over the head of punter Paul Burton was recovered in the end zone by Badger freshman walk-on Bob Adamov, giving Wisconsin a 7-0 lead just 1:16 into the game. The teams went back and forth from there, with the lead changing hands five times until a 2-yard run by Martin increased the Badger advantage to 30-20 with 13:31 remaining in the fourth quarter. Northwestern's Adrian Autry, substituting for Wildcat star tailback Darnell Autry who left the game with an injury to his right shoulder in the second quarter, scored from two yards out with 7:02 left to cut the Wisconsin lead to 30-27.

The Badgers (twice) and Wildcats (once) traded punts until Northwestern took over on its own 45-yard line with 2:23 left. Quarterback Steve Schnur completed a 17-yard pass to tight end Darren Drexler on first down, but three incompletions followed. That left Brian Gowins facing a 55-yard field goal attempt that he ended up missing to the left. The Badgers took over at their own 38 with 1:33 remaining.

"We were over on the sideline relaxing," Badger defensive back Jason Suttle said after the game. Little did anyone know the Wisconsin defense would be back on the field 44 seconds later.

Alvarez correctly said after the game and again many years later in his autobiography that the Badgers were not in a position to have Samuel take a knee without having to punt the ball back to Northwestern. "And the percentages are better handing the ball off than snapping for a punt on fourth down," the coach would write in *Don't Flinch*, his 2006 autobiography. Northwestern had demonstrated the risk inherent in snapping the ball on a punt way back in the first quarter of the game when Janus overshooting Burton gave the Badgers their first points of the day.

Dayne had enjoyed another fine afternoon. He had carried 26 times for a career-high 135 yards and one touchdown up to that point and had continued to solidify his spot as the Badgers' No. 1 tailback. Not only had he not lost a fumble that day, he had not lost a fumble in any of his 104 collegiate rushing attempts. Samuel handed to Dayne on first down and the freshman churned forward over right tackle for seven yards. Brad Nessler and Gary Danielson, the play-by-play man and analyst, respectively, for ESPN that day, talked at that point about two long streaks coming to an end: the Wildcats' 11-game conference winning streak and Darnell Autry's string of 19 consecutive 100-yard rushing efforts, ended by his injury earlier in the game.

But on second down and three Samuel took the snap from Derek Engler and turned to his left to hand the ball to Dayne. The exchange was never completed. Dayne didn't get a handle on the ball and it bounced to the turf where Wildcat safety Eric Collier recovered it. The second-guessing started immediately. Danielson, though neither he nor Nessler had suggested prior to the play that the Badgers should be taking a knee, questioned Alvarez's decision-making, asking on air, "Why are they even handing the ball off, you wonder?" Moments later, Danielson added, "It's the New York Giant-Joe Pisarcik play all over again," referencing the infamous moment in NFL lore when Pisarcik, the Giants' quarterback, fumbled a handoff to fullback Larry Csonka as New York was running out the clock in a 1978 game against the Philadelphia Eagles.

Northwestern took possession at the Wisconsin 41 and Schnur rushed for 21 yards before hitting wide receiver D'Wayne Bates on a 20-yard touchdown pass. The Badgers made a last-ditch come-back attempt that included a 30-yard swing pass to Dayne, but Samuel's final throw into the end zone was intercepted as time ran out.

Alvarez was heavily criticized not only by the ESPN announcers but by writers in the Camp Randall Stadium press box and others around the country who had watched the game on television. *Wisconsin State Journal* columnist Vic Feuerherd, like Danielson, used the Joe Pisarcik reference. ESPN's Lee Corso, a former college coach, also weighed in, claiming, "Alvarez lost the game. Alvarez should quit like Dickerson should," a reference to Temple coach Ron Dickerson, who had quit a couple weeks earlier.

Others, like Barnett and Michigan State coach Nick Saban, defended Alvarez. And Nessler later apologized to Alvarez, saying, "Anything we did that caused the Wisconsin coaching staff any undue criticism, on behalf of ESPN, if we blew it, we apologize, or at least I do. That's why you're coaching and we're in the booth. It's pretty easy up here."

Alvarez contended that he would make the same call if given another chance.

"If I had to do it over again, I would have run the same play and given the football to the same kid," Alvarez said. Dayne later thanked his coach for the show of support.

The Badgers had fallen to 0-3 in conference play after losing three straight games to nationally-ranked opponents by a total of just 10 points. They had to try to pick themselves up and regroup for a road game the next week at Michigan State, but they were unable to do it. Dayne was limited to 81 yards on just 15 carries (he played only until the midway point of the third quarter), while Michigan State freshman running back Sedrick Irvin rushed for 125 yards and a touchdown in a 30-13 Spartan win that dropped Wisconsin to 3-4 overall and 0-4 (for the first time since 1991) in Big Ten play. Just as they were being written off (Feuerherd wrote after the Michigan State loss that "the Badgers' hopes for a successful season died this day"), however, the Badgers dusted themselves off and, led by an incredible stretch of performances by Dayne, made a late-season run at a bowl bid.

Five regular-season games remained for Wisconsin when the calendar turned to November. The first was a date with Purdue in front of a home crowd in Madison and, with ESPN's Nessler and Danielson back in the booth, a national television audience looking on. Dayne entered the game ranked eighth in the Big Ten in rushing with a 90.3-yards-per-game average and 632 total yards, the second-most ever for a Wisconsin freshman behind only eventual Heisman Trophy winner Alan Ameche. His numbers were about to start rising quickly.

Dayne much preferred playing in cold weather, and the game-time temperature on November 2 at Camp Randall Stadium was 30 degrees. Dayne ran over, around and through the Boilermakers in the first half, accumulating 146 yards and two touchdowns on just 15 carries. He averaged 9.7 yards per attempt as the Badgers moved out to a 24-10 lead. Dayne had several memorable runs during his freshman season at Wisconsin. One was his amazing 12-yard score late in the game against Penn State. Another was the first of his two touchdowns against Purdue.

Thanks to Dayne's running and a 29-yard pass from Samuel to Donald Hayes, Wisconsin had moved to the Purdue 7-yard line midway through the first quarter. Samuel handed to Dayne up the middle for five yards to the 2, leaving the Badgers facing second and goal. Gibson, who had lined up at fullback for a play against Northwestern earlier in the season, was in the game as a second tight end (wearing No. 81) and lined up on the left side. When he was in the game with the Badgers' other linemen, Wisconsin's already massive offensive front grew to epic proportions, weighing in at 1,922 pounds. Tight end Kevin Lyles was lined up on the right side and fullback Cecil Martin was in front of Dayne. Lyles went in motion from right to left and Dayne again got the call. He carried around the left side. Lyles blocked linebacker Chike Okeafor, and Gibson and Co. completely sealed off the rest of Purdue's interior defenders. That left 199-pound strong safety Willie Burroughs just where the Badgers always wanted a defensive back: one on one with Dayne. Burroughs ran up and met Dayne at the 1-yard line, but the freshman, carrying the ball in his left hand and picking up momentum as he barreled toward the end zone, lowered his right shoulder and literally ran right over Burroughs. The Boilermaker ended up on his back with his feet straight up in the air as Dayne looked back to assess the damage before celebrating with his teammates.

Asked more than a decade later to recall a signature Dayne run, offensive lineman Bill Ferrario, then redshirting as a freshman, harkened back to that play. "If there was a dictionary [entry] that said 'Ron Dayne,' the video of that play should be next to it," said Ferrario, who would start for the last three years of Dayne's career. "That summed up Ron Dayne in a 10-second video clip."

Purdue closed to within 24–17 in the third quarter and 33–25 early in the fourth quarter, but that was the final. Dayne ended up with 244 yards and two touchdowns on 30 carries, a remarkable 8.1-yards-per-attempt average. He smashed Ameche's school single-game freshman rushing record of 200 yards (vs. Minnesota) that had stood since 1951. He also eclipsed Ameche's UW freshman rushing record (824 yards) for a season. Dayne's 244 yards were the second-most in a game in UW history behind Billy Marek's 304-yard effort against Minnesota in 1974. But he was, as Alvarez was fond of saying, "just getting lathered up."

The second chapter in Dayne's "November to Remember" brought arch-rival Minnesota to Madison on a cold, snowy Senior Day at Camp Randall Stadium. The Golden Gophers were the owners of a 12-game losing streak in conference play. Gopher head coach Jim Wacker was under fire. And, most ominous of all, Minnesota ranked 79th nationally in total defense, including 97th against the run. Given that set of circumstances, what transpired that day was not surprising. It was, however, awe-inspiring.

The Badgers rolled to a 28-7 halftime lead with Dayne doing practically all of the damage. He carried the ball on a remarkable 31 of Wisconsin's 41 first-half plays, accumulating 166 yards and three touchdowns. The 31 carries fell just three short of tying the NCAA record for rushing attempts in a half. Noticeable not only in the first half but throughout the game was the reluctance of the Minnesota defenders to square up and fully engage Dayne. Rather, the Gophers too often tried to arm-tackle the freshman or made what looked like half-hearted attempts to bring him down.

"I noticed that," Dayne said of Minnesota's would-be tacklers after the game. "After a while they'd start acting like they were going to tackle me, then dive towards the ground."

It was more of the same in the second half. The Badgers increased their lead to 42-13 as Dayne continued his assault. Alvarez took him out in the third quarter, but put him back in midway through the fourth quarter after the Gophers had cut the lead to 42-28. Dayne carried the ball on seven consecutive plays – the last attempt his NCAA freshman-record 50th of the game – on the Badgers' last scoring drive that ended with a Hall field goal and secured a 45-28 win. Dayne finished the game with 297 yards and three touchdowns. He was just the fifth back in Big Ten history to carry the ball at least 50 times in a game. His yardage total fell just seven yards shy of Marek's school mark and was the eighth-highest figure in conference history. It was also the third-best rushing performance by a freshman in NCAA history behind only San Diego State's Marshall Faulk (386) and Florida State's Greg Allen (322). Building upon his 244-yard effort of a week earlier against Purdue, Dayne had rushed for 541 total yards in consecutive games, eclipsing Marek's UW record of 534 yards.

"He just gets behind those big linemen and pounds at you," Wacker said afterward. "He's the toughest kid in the Big Ten to bring down. I don't think there is any doubt about that. He's for real."

Cecil Martin knew Dayne was for real, too. But that didn't mean his rookie backfield mate never got tired, particularly because he had so many carries.

"It was interesting because, in the beginning, he was running the ball a lot," the Badger fullback said of Dayne's early days at Wisconsin. "Forget that he was a big guy at 260 pounds; he was running the ball a lot. Sometimes he was so tired I'd have to let him know what the snap count was. There are pictures of me lined up in front of him with my hand behind my back actually showing him the snap count, one, two or three."

Once Dayne got going, however, Martin wasn't any more interested in getting in his way than opposing linebackers and defensive backs were.

"I like to tell people that part of the reason I even made it to the NFL was that I was more scared of him running into my back than the linebacker I had to block," Martin recalled. "One time I ran through the hole and hit a linebacker and he ran through my leg and it hurt so bad. I never wanted Ron Dayne running into my back ever again or running through my leg ever again. The thing that was great about blocking for him is that he had unbelievable vision. There would be times when we would be [watching] film and if you paused it, there was no hole there. If you kept going, the hole opened up. It was an uncanny instinct he had to know the flow of the defense and where the hole was."

Wisconsin had three regular-season games remaining, all on the road, against Iowa, Illinois and Hawaii. The Badgers were still in the hunt for a bowl bid when they traveled to Iowa City to meet the Hawkeyes on November 16. They had some momentum after the wins over Purdue and Minnesota, and they would be facing an Iowa team that had been hammered, 40-13, the week before by Northwestern. The Wildcats' Darnell Autry had rushed for 241 yards in the win. With Dayne running wild, perhaps this would be the year the Badgers knocked off the Hawkeyes for the first time since 1976. Or not.

A year earlier Ron Dayne had committed to attend Wisconsin after watching the Hawkeyes put the clamps on the Badgers' running game in a 33-20 Iowa win at Camp Randall Stadium. In that game, Iowa's Sedrick Shaw ran all over the Badgers for 214 yards and three touchdowns. The 1996 rematch at Iowa was an instant replay of sorts. The Hawkeyes routed the Badgers, 31-0, with Shaw picking up 143 yards and three touchdowns. On the other side of the ball, Samuel threw two interceptions and lost three fumbles. Dayne, who had been named the Big Ten Offensive Player of the Week for each of his two previous outings, rushed for just 62 yards – his lowest total since becoming the starter – and the Badgers accumulated only 128 yards in total offense. The forgettable performance extended the UW's winless streak against Iowa to 18 games, left the Badgers with a 5-5 overall record and in need of a win the next week at Illinois to keep their bowl hopes alive.

"Someday I'll be telling my grandchildren that I played with him," senior linebacker Pete Monty said of Dayne following yet another of the rookie's eye-popping efforts, this one coming in a 35-15 victory over the Fighting Illini. Media and teammates alike were running out of superlatives to describe Dayne, who gashed the Illinois defense for 289 yards and four touchdowns on 41 carries. He scored on runs of 30, 54, 19 and 23 yards. He carried on 22 of the Badgers' first 30 plays, helping Wisconsin build a 28-7 lead at the half behind his school-record (for rushing yards in a half) 212 yards.

Dayne's outlandish performances were starting to bring him into the company of some of college football's legends. His showing at Illinois moved his season rushing yardage total to 1,524, the third-most for a freshman in NCAA history behind only Pittsburgh star and 1976 Heisman Trophy winner Tony Dorsett and Georgia icon Herschel Walker. Dayne still had at least one game left to play, and he was only 113 yards behind the school season record of 1,637, set in 1993 by Brent Moss.

"The kid is a great athlete, and he has a lot of heart and he'll do anything to get yards — we appreciate a running back like him," right tackle Jerry Wunsch said at the time. "Dayne is still learning. That's the great thing about Ron. He doesn't even know how good he's going to be yet."

Whether Dayne knew it or not, opposing defenses certainly did. He had averaged an amazing 223 yards per game and scored nine touchdowns in four November contests. He had become just the fifth back in Big Ten history — freshman or otherwise — to rush for more than 1,300 yards in conference games. He had produced two of the top five rookie rushing efforts in NCAA history. He had twice gained 100 yards in a quarter. The list went on and on as the Badgers prepared to face Hawaii in their regular-season finale on November 30 with a bowl berth — most likely against Utah in the Copper Bowl in Tucson, Arizona — on the line.

The Rainbow Warriors were on the way to one of their worst seasons in school history (they brought a 2-9 record into their Senior Day game with Wisconsin). Hawaii was allowing 208.9 rushing yards per game, and none of its defensive starters weighed as much as Dayne, let alone the Badgers' massive offensive line. In fact, Dayne outweighed a couple of the Rainbow Warrior defensive backs by nearly 100 pounds. On paper, it looked like a mismatch, but Alvarez was concerned nonetheless. He didn't feel his team was focused on the task at hand as it made final preparations at practice the day before the game.

"We were going through our script of 15 openers, and we were on play No. 12 when I jumped the offense and made them start over from No. 1," Alvarez wrote in his autobiography. His nervousness turned out to be unfounded.

The game was not televised on the U.S. mainland so, aside from the two teams, the media, the game officials and the 26,819 fans inside Aloha Stadium that night, only those watching a local telecast in Hawaii were witness to Dayne's astonishing performance against the home team. The game started with four straight penalties, including an illegal motion call on the first play that negated a 67-yard run by Dayne. Once the flurry of penalties was over, he ran for 71 yards, with Hawaii defenders bouncing off him and hanging on for dear life, on his first official carry and scored from four yards out two plays later. Dayne went on to set a school record for rushing yards in a half with 250, to go with three touchdowns, on just 25 attempts for a 10-yards per carry average. On his final run of the first half, a 48-yard score, five Rainbow Warriors got a hand on him, but to no avail. Prior to the 1996 season, Dayne's 250-yard half would have been the second-best rushing performance ever for a Badger in a *full game*. Dayne added 89 more yards and another touchdown in the third quarter before Alvarez pulled him for good.

"Men and boys," Alvarez would say of Dayne's effort. "I didn't feel like we were ready to play and we go out and they flat wouldn't tackle him. By the middle of the third quarter he had 300-some yards. It was getting embarrassing. You'd hand him the ball and those guys were finding ways ... the secondary was just finding ways to disappear. If I'd left him in the game, he would've had over 500 yards."

It would have been easy for Alvarez to do just that, but he stuck to his personal philosophy about records that evening in Honolulu and, in the face of criticism from others, throughout Dayne's career as a Badger.

"I like to break records, but I think records should be broken in the context of the game," Alvarez said then and on several occasions in subsequent years. "There was no reason to put him in to go for an NCAA record. He broke the freshman rushing record, he broke the Wisconsin record and he's nearing 2,000 yards. We all know he's a very good back."

The Badgers went on to win the "must-win" game, 59-10, and set themselves up with an opportunity to take on Utah in the Copper Bowl, the school's third bowl game in four years.

"That game provided a good lesson that probably paid off down the road in that it was a big game for us and if we didn't win it, we were going home for the winter," McIntosh said. "I guess it was maybe just a dress rehearsal for some of the bigger games that were going to come the next couple years. I remember there were a lot of emotions in that game – it was the only game the offensive line ever got the game ball from, at least while I was there. I've got that ball on my bookshelf at home."

Dayne's 339-yard, four-touchdown romp at Hawaii smashed Marek's single-game school rushing mark that Dayne had been flirting with all month. He had passed Herschel Walker (by 247 yards) for first place on the NCAA's freshman rushing list. He had become the UW's single-season rushing leader with his 1,863-yard total. And he now had recorded (all in November) three of the six top rookie rushing games in NCAA history.

"What I remember during that stretch (in November of 1996) was that I had never spent so much time in the NCAA record book," then UW men's sports information director Malchow said. "I was grooming the rushing stats for as many things as I could find. I remember just looking at pure attempts. Tony Sands of Kansas had the record at the time. As a statistician or P.R. person, you're looking for little angles and they were not hard to come by. My only frustration was that the NCAA didn't have all their stats broken down by class because he would have broken all of them for a freshman. The stretch was just off the charts."

But Dayne's off-the-charts accomplishments didn't make the quiet freshman any more interested in talking about himself than he had been back on media day in August.

"I remember the Hawaii game his freshman year, when he ran for 339 yards and didn't want to do interviews after the game," Malchow said. "We were on major deadline because the game was in Hawaii (it ended around 2 a.m. central time) and he had just broken the school's rushing record in one of the most phenomenal performances I had ever seen and he didn't understand why the media wanted to talk to him. That was pretty interesting as the P.R. person."

There was, however, one topic he would discuss: his offensive line. Throughout his career, Dayne unfailingly credited the Badgers up front who opened holes for him. The majority of the 1996 line only played one year with Dayne, but there was a clear camaraderie. In fact, in the weeks before the Copper Bowl against Utah Dayne presented the unit with t-shirts as a show of appreciation for their role in his record-breaking campaign. The shirts read: O-line, My Kind of People, My Kind of Guys. It was a show of gratitude that became typical of Dayne during his time at Wisconsin and it wasn't always reserved just for the offensive linemen. The freshman even signed a photo of himself, had it framed and brought it along with him on the plane to Tucson for the Copper Bowl. He stopped at Alvarez's hotel room during the trip and gave his coach the gift in appreciation for the way Alvarez had welcomed him and treated him. Dayne would have bigger gifts to give in the coming years.

Hawaii defensive coordinator Don Lindsey said after the game against the Badgers that facing Dayne "was like trying to stop a Mack truck with a pea shooter. It was no contest." The focus of all the attention as the Badgers prepared to face head coach Ron McBride's Utah Utes, however, was on not one Mack truck, but two. Dayne weighed in at 5-10, 260 pounds, but he wasn't the largest tailback in the nation in 1996. That honor went to Utah sophomore Chris Fuamatu-Ma'afala, who was listed at 6-1, 276. Fuamatu-Ma'afala had missed three games with an injury, but still managed 982 rushing yards and nine touchdowns for the Utes, who finished 8-3 overall. *USA Today* ran a story previewing the matchup as "The Great Dayne" challenging "The Polynesian Pulverizer" in a "Copper Bowl confrontation of earthshaking proportions." It had all the makings of an interesting matchup until Fuamatu-Ma-afala injured his ankle early in the first half with just five yards rushing on four carries. The spotlight shone solely on Dayne after that.

The Badgers went up 7-3, thanks to a 38-yard touchdown run by Samuel early in the first quarter. Then as Fuamatu-Ma'afala was being helped to a golf cart on the Utah sideline, his ankle wrapped in ice, Dayne put together runs of 37 and 40 yards (the second one a touchdown) to reach the century mark on just his seventh carry. It was the fifth time in the past three games that Dayne had rushed for 100 yards in a quarter and the touchdown run, in particular, showed Dayne's rare combination of speed, power, vision and agility. On the play, he carried over left tackle, made a sharp cut to the right in front of safety Harold Lusk (whose over-pursuit left him helplessly out of position once Dayne switched direction) and ran past cornerback Clarence Lawson. Dayne finished the run in the right corner of the end zone after starting his run near the left hash mark.

ESPN's Gary Danielson, joined on the game telecast by Brad Nessler, said after the play: "When they say Ron Dayne runs smart … he runs with his eyes. I don't know if there is a fair comparison to him, as to what he is as a running back. He's just stocky enough to use his weight smartly. I think he's different than even a Jerome Bettis or Ironhead (Heyward). I just can't think of anyone that matches up to the way he's built or the way he runs." Nessler added, "Someday we might be looking at a guy that they say, 'You know, he runs like Ron Dayne.'"

Wisconsin rolled to a 31-3 halftime lead before finishing the job in a 38-10 victory. Dayne was named the game's MVP after accumulating a UW bowl-record 246 yards rushing on 30 carries to go along with three touchdowns. The performance allowed him to break the Big Ten season rushing record previously held by Michigan State's Lorenzo White.

Dayne ended his freshman campaign with 2,109 yards rushing and 21 touchdowns on 325 carries, all school records at the time. He joined a group of 10 other players in college football history to have rushed for 2,000 yards in a season (bowl games included). He set the NCAA freshman record for rushing attempts in a season with 295 (bowl game not included). He finished fourth nationally with a 162.2 yards-per-game averaged and averaged 195.8 yards per contest as a starter. The numbers were mind-boggling. Dayne even finished 13th in the Heisman Trophy voting. And he didn't start until the fifth game of the season.averaged 195.8 yards per contest as a starter. The numbers were mind-boggling. Dayne even finished 13th in the Heisman Trophy voting. And he didn't start until the fifth game of the season.

CHAPTER FIVE
The Great Dayne

Barry Alvarcz always preached "team first" and that approach proved successful over his 16-year head coaching career at Wisconsin. The Badger football program under his direction wasn't given to hyperbole or glitzy promotional campaigns. Individual success, he believed, came with team success. He often talked about eliminating distractions. Alvarez thought all along that Ron Dayne could be a special player, and Dayne proved him right with his remarkable freshman season in 1996. But Alvarez never really went overboard in his praise of Dayne nor singled out the freshman. Instead, he simply acknowledged the prized rookie's accomplishments and, like everyone else, expressed amazement and admiration.

Given Alvarez's customary approach, it may have seemed out of character for him to have made the following pronouncement after Dayne had steamrolled Utah for 246 yards and three touchdowns in the 1996 Copper Bowl: "They keep talking about [Dayne] for the Heisman, and there's no reason he shouldn't be right in the mix. No freshman has ever done what Dayne has done, and there aren't many who have ever rushed for 2,000 yards." Alvarez was correct. No freshman had ever done what Dayne did in 1996, and the numbers alone were reason enough for him to be part of the Heisman conversation. But that conversation involved more than just playing football.

Once he was able to take a postseason break from researching new Dayne records, Badger men's sports information director Steve

Malchow took some time to contemplate what a run at the Heisman Trophy might look like for Dayne. He knew Alvarez would want a plan of some kind. He knew that with a Heisman Trophy candidate comes increased media attention and that wouldn't exactly be in Dayne's wheelhouse. But he also knew that players like Dayne came along once in a generation and the benefits – for the university, the football program and for Dayne himself – of winning a Heisman Trophy, or at least being in the Heisman race, could last for years.

Malchow decided in the spring of 1997 to bring in Andrea Kirby, a nationally-recognized media relations consultant, to visit with UW athletics administrators, coaches and athletes, particularly Dayne.

"I remember," Malchow said, "after the one-on-one session (that Kirby did with Dayne), she just came up to me and said, 'He is just a delightful kid, really, really nice kid. Good luck'. I asked her what she meant by 'good luck.' She said, 'You're going to have to work hard to get the key to that lock because he is very guarded with his comments and it's going to essentially end up falling on the trust factor. I hope you earn his trust because that's really where it has to start and then you can guide him along.'"

Shelly Poe, Malchow's counterpart at West Virginia University, suggested that Malchow find something Dayne felt comfortable discussing, something about which he could easily communicate. That something turned out to be dogs.

"I tried to take inventory of Ron's personality," Malchow said. "He was by far the quietest superstar I'd ever worked with. I knew he wasn't going to want to do the speakers circuit and I needed to find a way to keep his name out there."

Dayne's last name got Malchow thinking about Great Danes and about Dane County, where Madison is located. He initially thought that if he decided to do something with Great Danes, the star tailback might be able to hold a Great Dane puppy under his arm like a football. That was until he saw the size of a young Great Dane. So, Malchow took a different direction. He called Dayne to his office and told him he was looking for an off-the-field activity he could get the running back involved with. Malchow stressed to Dayne that whatever it was had to be legitimate and true to who Dayne was. He asked the running back if he liked dogs.

"Ron said he loved dogs and that he and his sister, Onya, had dogs when they were growing up," Malchow recalled. "Ron said his was named Butch and Onya's was named Fluffy. That gave me the motivation to pursue a relationship with the Dane County Humane Society. The person I worked with at the Humane Society probably about fell out of her chair when I contacted her. Here I had one of the most famous people in Madison volunteering his time to push her cause. For a P.R. person at a non-profit, that's pretty much hitting the jackpot."

Mary Paul Long, then the director of development and public relations for the Dane County Humane Society, was indeed enthusiastic. "I was, of course, thrilled," Long said at a July news conference unveiling the effort that was equal parts public service initiative and Heisman Trophy campaign. "The Humane Society is in the business of adopting animals. This is the first time we've been adopted."

Humane Society posters, featuring Dayne and four Great Danes, were distributed throughout Dane County. The tailback did public service announcements and made some public appearances, including an event at the governor's residence, all in the name of the "Humane Treatment of Animals, Not Linebackers!" It was a clever and substantive project that kept Dayne in the public eye in a way that was comfortable for him.

Dayne had other off-the-field matters to attend to as well. His girlfriend, Alia Lester, whom he had met the summer prior to his freshman year, was pregnant. She would give birth to the couple's first child on November 3, 1997.

Things were evolving off the field for Dayne, but changes were also occurring within the Wisconsin football program. Senior-to-be running back Carl McCullough, who went from starting to averaging only six carries per game over the team's final six contests in 1996, was reported to have decided to declare for early entry into the NFL draft. McCullough, who had approached Alvarez weeks earlier about a potential position switch so he could get on the field in some capacity, ultimately remained in the program for his final year. Junior-to-be Aaron Stecker, however, decided to transfer. Much like McCullough, Dayne's emergence had resulted in decreased playing time at running back for Stecker, although he did establish himself as the Big Ten's fourth-leading punt returner as a sophomore. Stecker said at the time, "Every kid who plays football dreams of making it to the NFL, to have a chance. I want to know I did everything possible to have a chance at that." Stecker moved on to star at Western Illinois where he became the school's career rushing leader before enjoying a lengthy career as a multi-purpose player in the NFL.

Another change for the Badgers early in 1997 involved the team's schedule. A non-conference slate that included Boise State, San Jose State and San Diego State was bolstered by the addition of Syracuse, whom Wisconsin signed to play in the Kickoff Classic in Giants Stadium on August 24. The game against the Orangemen, whose roster included Heisman Trophy contending quarterback Donovan McNabb, would be a homecoming for Dayne and several other Badgers from the area. It would also aid in early publicity for the Badger sophomore's Heisman Trophy hopes.

Perhaps the most significant change in the program – the one that would most directly affect Dayne's performance – was the departure of Vanderveldt, Castro, Wunsch and Engler, the four senior offensive linemen who, with the redshirt freshman McIntosh, were largely responsible for opening the holes through which Dayne ran during his record-breaking rookie season. Heading into spring practice in 1997, the Badgers' plan was to insert Aaron Gibson into the right tackle spot, while taking a look at junior college transfer Coleman Johnson and redshirt freshmen Dave Costa and Jason Eck at center and redshirt freshmen like Costa, Casey Rabach, Bill Ferrario, Joe Gribowski and Nick Bradley at the guard positions. McIntosh, who started all 13 games as a redshirt freshman in 1996, was the "wily veteran."

McIntosh had come to the Badgers from Pewaukee, a small community about 20 minutes west of Milwaukee. The town did not have a youth football program when McIntosh was growing up, so he did not put on a pair of shoulder pads until he was a freshman at Pewaukee High School.

"I don't think I was that great of a high school football player as much as I was just stronger than everybody else," McIntosh said. "I was an offensive and defensive lineman and played on special teams. My junior and senior year I don't think I ever came out of the game. It was a small high school so you just did what you had to do."

McIntosh started attending Alvarez's University of Wisconsin football camps the summer after his sophomore year. The following fall the Badgers burst onto the college football scene by winning the Big Ten championship and the Rose Bowl, exciting McIntosh about the prospects of possibly playing in Madison. Alvarez offered McIntosh a scholarship during the summer of 1994, a few months before he was to start his senior year.

"I remember my mom picking me up from the (UW football) camp that day and driving back to Pewaukee," McIntosh said. "I said, 'Well, they want me to come to school here.' She kind of smiled and was happy about it, but she didn't really have the reaction I thought she would. And I said, 'No, Mom, they want to give me a scholarship to come to school here and play football!' All the way home, it was like we were walking on clouds – it was just a surreal moment."

Though schools like Michigan and Notre Dame were also pursuing McIntosh, he accepted Alvarez's scholarship offer that included a promise by the coach to honor the offer if McIntosh were to sustain an injury during his senior year at Pewaukee. McIntosh ended up needing Alvarez's insurance policy because he tore the anterior cruciate ligament (ACL) in his right knee early in his senior season. The injury required three surgeries that fall, and McIntosh's recovery was slowed by a serious staph infection that resulted in a three-week hospital stay and what McIntosh remembers to be about a 50-pound weight loss.

"That was a really tough time; I didn't know if I would play again," McIntosh said. "At a point they were worried about how bad the infection was. Before they got in there, they were worried about saving my leg in general because the staph infection was so bad. It was pretty serious and all I was worried about was if I could play football. I guess that's not really what I should have been worried about. I give Barry a lot of credit for sticking to that offer. He certainly didn't have to, that's for sure."

McIntosh recovered and, although he never played that first year, ended up making the Badgers' travel squad as a true freshman. It taught him how to travel and prepare for a game, and it gave him time to spend with and learn from the team's veteran offensive linemen.

"It was all I could do just to hold onto my hat that first year, just to figure out where to go and what was expected of me," McIntosh recalled. The Badger coaches were already recognizing the leadership potential in McIntosh in the spring of 1997.

"I think Mac understands what it was like as a (starting) red-shirt freshman and the old-timers taking him under their wings," Alvarez said at the time, referring to the likes of Castro, Engler,

Vanderveldt and Wunsch. "He hung out with those guys and spent a lot of time with them. He knows what they were all about. Those guys did a nice job of leading us. So, he knows how to do it."

The Badgers' young line got even younger in an unfortunate twist of fate a week before the team's spring game. Johnson, who had been starting at center and had set a couple UW conditioning records, tore his ACL in the team's 11th practice of the spring. He was projected to be out until at least October, but he never did suit up for the Badgers. That left Alvarez and his staff with a very green starting unit, but whose members would become household names to Wisconsin football fans in the coming years: McIntosh at left tackle, Ferrario at left guard, Rabach at center, Costa at right guard and Gibson at right tackle. That group, with the occasional exception, would start together for the next two years.

Spring turned to summer and the hype that surrounds the Heisman Trophy race began. The widely acknowledged front-runner for the award was Tennessee quarterback Peyton Manning, who was the top returning vote-getter after finishing eighth in the balloting in 1996. Dayne, who got eight votes to finish 13th in the Heisman race after his stunning freshman season, was the No. 2 returning vote-getter. Dayne and Manning had met in the spring when the two were in Phoenix for *Playboy* magazine's All-America weekend and photo shoot.

Playboy was not the only publication interested in Dayne. He made the cover of several preseason college football magazines, including one – *Preview Sports* – that posed the headline question: "The Best Running Back of All Time?" Others included *Athlon's*, *Lindy's*, *The Sporting News* and *Inside Sports*. Later in the summer, newspapers like the *New York Times, New York Daily News*, the *Washington Post, USA Today* and the *Philadelphia Inquirer* ran lengthy feature stories on Dayne. In late July Dayne and Badger linebacker David Lysek attended the Big Ten Football Media Days in Chicago where they spent 48 hours doing interviews with media from all over the Midwest and the nation. Thanks to the work of Malchow, Kirby and Dayne's involvement with the Dane County Humane Society, however, the running back was at least feeling more comfortable with the notion that everyone wanted to talk to him.

"I feel more relaxed because I'm used to some of the questions they come at me with," Dayne told the *Wisconsin State Journal*'s Andy Baggot that summer. "Being able to go through the whole season (in 1996) being interviewed, I guess you can't do anything but get better or start to like it. One or the other, you've got to do something."

Though cautious about Dayne becoming overwhelmed, Alvarez embraced the opportunity to have one of his players in the thick of the Heisman Trophy chatter. In fact, the second paragraph of Dayne's biographical profile in the 1997 Badger football media guide contained the lines "one of the leading candidates for the 1997 Heisman Trophy and Maxwell Award" and "trying to become the first sophomore in history to win the Heisman Trophy."

Fall camp opened early for the Badgers in 1997 because they were opening the season earlier than they ever had. One of the news items that came from preseason workouts that year was the naming of team captains Kevin Huntley, Lysek and McCullough, whose selection by his teammates demonstrated the respect they had for him and the unselfish role he assumed as Dayne bypassed him on the depth chart. McCullough expressed surprise. Alvarez did not.

"Carl has earned all his respect with the way he has handled this situation," Alvarez said at the time. "He never pouted and has always been there to help other people."

The 24th-ranked Badgers and 17th-ranked Syracuse finally opened the 1997 college football season on the afternoon of August 24. ABC carried the game to a national audience with

Nessler and Danielson handling the commentary. Hyping the Dayne-McNabb matchup right from the start, the telecast began with clips highlighting each player's achievements and memorable plays from a year earlier. Cameras also showed a sizeable group of family and friends in attendance to support the Badger sophomore. It was a much-anticipated matchup between two nationally-ranked teams with two marquee players. There was only one problem: one of the marquee players was hurt.

Dayne had sustained a "stinger," an injury to the neck and shoulder, during training camp. He had been held out of contact for several days, though he told reporters after the game that he had regained some of the strength in the area in the days leading up to the season opener.

"We had a veteran offensive line (when Dayne was a freshman) where he could anticipate the combination blocks," Alvarez recalled years later. "We had Wunsch, Vanderveldt – that's an NFL line. Those guys came off blocks, you knew and trusted their combinations. All of a sudden the next year we've got all these young guys and we're running a middle drill and [Dayne] anticipated somebody coming off and a defender smacks him and gives him a stinger. He had that stinger all through camp and he was wearing that big collar and couldn't move his neck. And Syracuse was just flat-out a lot better than us. That was one of the more talented teams I saw my whole career at Wisconsin."

ABC sideline reporter Dean Blevins informed Nessler and Danielson on the air moments before kickoff that Dayne was indeed wearing a protective collar and said Dayne had been held out of contact during practice for 11 days due to the stinger.

Syracuse's Kevin Johnson took Vitaly Pisetsky's opening kickoff 89 yards for a touchdown and the Orangemen never looked back. They led 24-0 at halftime and cruised to a 34-0 victory. Dayne carried only 13 times for 46 yards, the lowest rushing total of his career at that point. Wisconsin gained just 223 yards of total offense, including only 60 on the ground, and allowed 470 total yards to McNabb and the Orangemen. McNabb completed 11 of 14 passes for 211 yards, throwing for one touchdown and running for another. The postgame media coverage focused on McNabb outplaying Dayne, but Alvarez defended his running back.

"I said before the game that Ron Dayne was not a one-man wrecking crew," Alvarez said. "We better have people who can block for him and create seams for him to run in. He got the maximum out of what was blocked."

It was clear the Badgers, particularly the offensive line, had work to do. But it was a group willing to put in that work.

"When we got thumped at Syracuse – when they were all redshirt freshmen – they weren't very popular at that time," said Jim Hueber, the team's offensive line coach, referring to Ferrario, Costa and Rabach. "We knew they had talent, but we knew we were in one of those lulls where we had to get game experience for them. They wound up having a helluva year; they won eight games and went to a bowl. I remember they all really, really wanted to play. They were guys that were really into it. They were guys that really thought more about the game than it being just a pastime. It really was a vocation for them."

McIntosh recalled the difficult beginning the three new interior linemen had.

"I remember that first camp with Bill, Dave and Casey – that was a rough camp and that was a tough year," McIntosh said. "We had to scrap to get to a decent bowl game. We were very, very young and made some mistakes that go along with having a young O-line. In camp there were some concerns about how this was going to come together and if we had the right mix of guys. Then, the longer we played together, the better we played and you just got to the point where you could trust that the other guy was going to be where he was supposed to be. It just built and built to the point where my last year with Bill – it got to the point where we didn't make vocal calls – we had our own little system of communicating."

Ferrario, too, has vivid recollections of his early days as the Badgers tried to put together a line that could open holes for Dayne and protect Samuel.

"That first year Chris McIntosh was the only one with experience on the offensive line and I think he only had 13 games under his belt," Ferrario said. "It was a little shaky. Chris, as young as he was, was an excellent leader on the field. Coach Hueber, you couldn't ask for a better coach, especially with the situation he had with three guys who had never stepped foot on a college field and only one guy that had played a full season, but was still young. I think we definitely took a couple years off of Coach Hueber's life in '97, with the mistakes and trying to make adjustments, but he definitely got us to pull together and play, all five of us, as a unit of one."

Rabach's recollection of that time is similar.

"Coach Hueber never pulled any punches," Rabach said. "He gave it to you straight and told you what he thought. It may not have been what you wanted to hear, but it was the truth and that's all you could ask for. It was nice to have two other guys there in the same situation at the time to lean on and share the experiences with and it made for a really tight friendship with those two guys."

A unit of one is just what the three redshirt freshmen – Ferrario, Rabach and Costa – became. They started in the middle of the Badgers' offensive line for four straight seasons, the first three with Dayne in the backfield and the last one with Dayne's successor, Michael Bennett, playing tailback. They each took a different road to Madison, but together they formed relationships that last to this day.

Rabach, who starred at Sturgeon Bay High School under the tutelage of his father, Gary, the team's offensive line coach, had attended the University of Iowa's football camp and had, in fact, been offered a scholarship by the Hawkeyes. But Rabach also took part in the Badgers' camp and was eventually offered a scholarship to come to Madison.

"It was definitely an easy decision to choose Wisconsin, being my home state and knowing guys on the team already with a few local guys down there and with the coaching staff that they had," Rabach said.

Rabach was an honorable mention high school All-American according to *USA Today*, a first-team all-state choice and his conference's player of the year.

Ferrario grew up in Scranton, Pennsylvania, participating in Cub Scouts (he later became an Eagle Scout) and spending much of his time playing baseball in part because, at 9 or 10 years old, he was too big to play football with other boys his age. Though baseball was his passion, Ferrario's coach convinced him to give football a try as he was entering high school. Ferrario found he enjoyed the gridiron every bit as much as the baseball diamond, and by his junior year in high school, he was being recruited by a number of colleges in his region, including Penn State.

"It came down to crunch time and Penn State actually stopped recruiting me," Ferrario said. "Being from that tri-state area (Pennsylvania, New York, New Jersey), everybody pretty much wants to go to Penn State, but they stopped recruiting me, so I started recruiting Penn State, and the last phone call I had with them was just as Wisconsin was coming into the mix. Penn State had told me they didn't think I was big enough or tough enough to be a Big Ten football player. At the time, Coach Hueber had been talking with me about getting me out on an official visit and once Penn State said that ... if I wasn't going to play for them I wanted to play against them and Wisconsin was the perfect school of choice. They had beaten Penn State my senior year of high school and I took the visit and I don't think we were off the plane for 10 minutes when I told my mom that if Coach Alvarez offered, I was going to say yes, no questions asked. That went well and Coach offered me, I accepted and came out to Wisconsin in '96."

Ferrario had been recruited as a defensive lineman and redshirted as such during his freshman year. But with the departures of Wunsch, Vanderveldt and the others, Ferrario was moved to the other side of the line of scrimmage prior to spring practice in 1997.

Like Ferrario, Costa was from Pennsylvania (Ellwood City, near the Pennsylvania-Ohio border between Pittsburgh and Youngstown) and, like Rabach, his father was a football coach (at Geneva College), in addition to having played football at Notre Dame. Costa was being recruited by UW assistant coach Jay Hayes.

"I had heard of the state of Wisconsin but I had never given any thought to Wisconsin football or even much about the state, coming from Pennsylvania," Costa said. "So I just went through the whole recruiting process like everybody else and I actually visited North Carolina State first and then went to Wisconsin. It was just a good place. I just kind of said, 'Alright, I'm going to go to Wisconsin.'"

It was a trio united by common experiences on the field and off, and those experiences helped forge lifelong bonds.

"The three of us were kind of inseparable all through college," Rabach said. "We lived together, we had a lot of the same classes. If one was somewhere, the other two weren't far behind. We stay in contact with each other still today. Not only was it a great relationship on the field, but off the field, too."

For Costa, the time they spent together on the field, at home, in class or studying game film brought them closer.

"I think first it was just kind of a situation of convenience because we were all kind of young offensive linemen," Costa said. "We spent a lot of time together and it just built into a relationship with the three of us – McIntosh, too, Mark Tauscher, even Gibson, we were all around each other. But Bill, Casey and I were kind of the closest of the three. I think that helped a lot on the field too – we were beside each other, a center and two guards, and having a close relationship helped a lot. It was just easy to be around each other so that made it easy to study film and that made it easier to work out and go to practice every day. So that helped a lot."

Ferrario's good fortune in the building of the relationships with the others was helped in part because he started out on the defensive line.

"When I came out to Wisconsin, I couldn't have asked for a better situation than to be roomed with Rabach," Ferrario recalled. "We were roommates at the seminary and that was the first time I had met him because I had not come out for that summer. Coach Alvarez's deal at the time was rooming offensive and defensive linemen together. I became really good friends with [Rabach] and that goes back, too, to the type of athletes Wisconsin recruited, the character. Myself, Dave and Casey, we were all the same type of people who grew up in different towns. We became friends instantly and a lot of it had to do with all of us being thrown into the mix at the same time, being yelled at, making mistakes, having to study more, having to practice more, so we all became close. We've remained lifelong friends and we all stay in touch and get together when our schedules allow. Casey and I roomed together for the first two years and me and Dave roomed together for the next three years. On flights, I pretty much sat with Dave and Casey was across the aisle from us. I roomed with Dave on the road, but Casey was always in our hotel room. We were pretty much inseparable our whole time at Wisconsin."

Given the intense scrutiny and fickle nature of Heisman Trophy analysis, there was no doubt that Dayne's Heisman Trophy hopes had taken a hit as a result of the loss at Syracuse.

The fact that Manning tied a school record with five touchdown passes in less than three quarters in a 52-17 win over Texas Tech on August 30 didn't help, either. But the Badgers were more concerned with getting Dayne healthy, making corrections and focusing on their September 6 home-opener against Boise State, a program just in its second year on the NCAA Division I level. The Broncos, coached by Houston Nutt, had lost 63-23 the previous week to Cal State-Northridge and most observers were predicting a one-sided Wisconsin victory with or without Dayne.

As it turned out, Dayne's biggest impact that day at Camp Randall came in the form of thousands of Dane County Humane Society posters featuring Dayne and four Great Danes that were given away as part of the running back's support of the Humane Society. Dayne was held out as his "stinger" continued to heal, leaving McCullough with his first start in nearly a year. Things did not begin well. The senior fumbled on the first play of the game and Boise State's Jeff Davis returned the ball 33 yards for a touchdown. The game did not go as predicted, but McCullough ran for 170 yards and a touchdown, while Samuel scored the winning touchdown on a 12-yard run with 49 seconds left. It was the first game Dayne had missed as a Badger.

He returned to action with a vengeance one week later when the Badgers traveled to San Jose State. The Spartans had one starter on defense who weighed more than Dayne and it showed. Dayne took a handoff from Samuel on the game's first play from scrimmage, went around the left side and down the San Jose State sideline for an 80-yard touchdown run, the longest of his UW career. On the play he outran at least three Spartan players. He went on to carry for 254 yards and three touchdowns on just 20 carries for an unbelievable 12.7-yards-per-carry average that day.

"Dayne is bigger than we saw on film," said San Jose State linebacker Josh Parry, who was unable to catch Dayne on his opening touchdown run. "He's a little quicker and faster for someone 260 pounds."

The 56-10 rout of the Spartans was followed by a 36-10 victory at home over San Diego State the following week. Dayne put up 145 yards and a career high-tying four touchdowns on 26 carries against the Aztecs. The Badgers were 3-1 after their rough start against Syracuse and were set to face Indiana at Camp Randall Stadium in the Big Ten opener on September 27, almost a year to the day of Dayne's breakout game against Penn State.

A headline in the *Wisconsin State Journal* on September 28, 1997, referred to another "ho-hum" day for Dayne. A day earlier he had ground out 202 yards (his UW record sixth 200-yard game) and a pair of touchdowns on 34 attempts to help lead the Badgers to a 27-26 win over Indiana. Matt "Money" Davenport booted a 43-yard field goal with six seconds left to give Wisconsin the victory. The Badgers won again the following week at Northwestern when Davenport connected from 48 yards out with six seconds left for a 26-25 win. The lead changed hands six times in the victory at Northwestern, and Samuel guided the Badgers to a fourth-quarter comeback win for the third time in six games. This time he took Wisconsin from its 4-yard line to the Northwestern 30 in the final 75 seconds of the game to set up Davenport's winner. Samuel threw for a career-high 271 yards that night in Evanston.

Mike Samuel ranked second in career pass completions (390) and third in career passing yards (4,989) and attempts (711) at Wisconsin upon completing his college career after the 1998 season. His 27 victories as a starting quarterback tied Darrell Bevell's school record, later broken by Brooks Bollinger. These figures may seem surprising since Samuel was never known for his ability to throw the football. He had a knack for completing passes when the Badgers needed a completion and he could throw the deep ball, but Samuel's real value to the Badgers was reflected in some of the intangibles that can't be coached. Samuel, a native of Philadelphia, was physically and mentally tough and was as good a leader as any of the other Alvarez-era quarterbacks like Bevell, Bollinger or John Stocco. Like the Badgers' running game during the Dayne years, Samuel wasn't flashy. He was not afraid to lower his shoulder and make contact with an opposing defender. Samuel gave the Badgers a viable running threat when the team ran the option, and his physical, no-nonsense style fit perfectly with the program's modus operandi.

Samuel also was a terrific leader. A tremendous amount of media attention invariably comes to the quarterback of any football team, and Samuel handled the post-game news conferences like he played: no frills, all business, say what needs to be said and get out. He certainly wasn't a reporter's dream. He wasn't wordy. But he often took personal responsibility for things that went wrong on the field, the most notable example being the infamous fumbled exchange between him and Dayne near the end of the 1996 Northwestern loss. Samuel said after that game, "We run that play a thousand times in practice. We didn't make the exchange and that's my fault." That kind of stand-up approach earned Samuel the respect of his coaches and teammates.

"The toughness he brought to the team was unbelievable," assistant coach and fellow Philadelphian Jim Hueber once said of Samuel. "His leadership qualities, the things other players told me after he left about how he handled himself and the team in the huddle were probably things people didn't see because he wasn't an outspoken guy."

The clutch play of Samuel and Davenport had helped the Badgers to five straight victories after the opening loss to Syracuse. Next up for Wisconsin was winless Illinois. Dayne had put together one of his outlandish November performances against the Fighting Illini a year earlier when he carried 41 times for 289 yards and four touchdowns. He wouldn't match those numbers in the 1997 contest, but he wasn't far off. Dayne piled up 207 rushing yards on only 28 attempts (a 7.4 yards-per-carry average) and a pair of touchdowns as the Badgers rolled to a 31-7 victory. Samuel added 85 yards through the air and a career-best 72 yards on the ground. Wisconsin was 6-1 overall, 3-0 in the Big Ten and, by Monday, would find itself ranked 24th nationally by the Associated Press with a key game at Purdue looming the next Saturday.

Many in the media had written Dayne off as a Heisman Trophy contender after the 34-0 loss to Syracuse at the Meadowlands. But the performance against Illinois prompted the noted national college football pundit Ivan Maisel to declare Dayne back in the race in a short piece he wrote for *Sports Illustrated* in the days following the win over Illinois. Calling attention to Dayne's 947 yards and 13 touchdowns in just six games, Maisel called the sophomore "a hybrid of an 18-wheeler and a Corvette." He also noted Dayne's humble demeanor on the field, quoting Illinois linebacker David James who said: "He'll run over you and run back to the huddle. That's the worst kind of opponent." Back on the Heisman radar, Dayne and the Badgers prepared not for the worst kind of opponent, but rather, a new kind.

Joe Tiller's entrance onto the Big Ten stage as Purdue's first-year head coach in 1997 not only helped introduce the spread offense into a conference whose style had long been marked by toughness and physical play as opposed to the wide-open, pass-happy philosophy of the spread, but it also signaled what would become a string of spellbinding and highly entertaining games between the Badgers and Boilermakers over the next decade. This initial matchup between Tiller and the Badgers, however, was not one of those games.

Dayne, despite what was reported to be a sore knee sustained in the first quarter, got his yards, rushing 26 times for 141 yards and a touchdown. But Purdue jumped out to a quick 21-0 lead, leaving the Badgers to abandon their ball-control offense. The Boilermakers went on to a 45-20 victory behind 559 yards of total offense.

Wisconsin – and Dayne – bounced back the following week, however, in a 22-21 win at Minnesota. Dayne, who a week earlier at Purdue had become just the 14th NCAA Division IA player to rush for 1,000 yards in his freshman and sophomore years, churned out 183 yards and one touchdown on 40 carries in his first appearance at the Metrodome in Minncapolis. Alvarez had said before the season that he had no plans to hand Dayne the ball as much as he did in November of 1996. Indeed, this was the last time Dayne reached the 40-carry mark in his collegiate career. He scored the game's winning touchdown in the fourth quarter and helped the Badgers run out the final 4:47 to preserve the one-point lead he had given them. In two games against Wisconsin's border rival to the west, Dayne had 90 rushing attempts for 480 yards and four scores. He again left the Golden Gophers amazed.

"He's a load," Gophers linebacker Parc Williams said after the game. "Until you get on the field and try to tackle him, you have no idea just how big and how strong he is. He gets so low to the ground, and he does a good job of going forward after you hit him."

The yards Dayne gained, as Williams said, "after you hit him" became known as "YAC" yards. YAC stood for Yards After Contact and it was a statistic that UW sports information director Steve Malchow maintained throughout Dayne's career. The figure was used quite often by the media because it was unique. It wasn't just a rushing average or a string of 100-yard games. It actually helped underline not just how tough and durable Dayne was, but also how difficult he was for opposing tacklers to bring down. Dayne finished his Badger career with 3,567 yards after contact, which at the time would have ranked third on the all-time Wisconsin rushing list.

The victory over Minnesota kept the Badgers, 7-2 overall, 4-1 in the Big Ten, on the radar screen as they looked ahead to a November 8 battle at home against Iowa. Five days before the game with the Hawkeyes, Dayne's girlfriend, Alia Lester, gave birth to the couple's first child, Jada, who weighed seven pounds, 13 ounces upon her arrival at Madison's Meriter Hospital. Caring for a baby certainly made life interesting for the two college sophomores.

"I was not sure how this was going to work," Alia said. "But luckily, it focused me. It just focused me [to get through school]. I scheduled all my classes, whether I liked them or not, I would just schedule my classes on Tuesdays and Thursdays and go to school on Tuesdays and Thursdays and my Grandpa, Jada's great grandpa, and Ron would alternate watching her. Or Ron watched her in the morning until he had to go to class and practice and then my grandpa would come in and watch her. Then, when that didn't work out for a while, I had some scholarship money and I would pay the neighbor two doors down to watch her. So it worked out, but it definitely focused me."

Jada, whose favorite two words later became 'Touchdown, Daddy,' gave Dayne something in common with his position coach, Brian White. Both were fathers of young children, and White came to admire the way Dayne handled fatherhood.

"I'm just really proud of the way he embraced fatherhood," White said. "How do I make that statement? If you've ever met his daughter, Jada, she was always such a happy kid. She went to the same pre-school as my daughter – they were a couple months apart. And Jada always had a spring in her step, always had a smile, was a happy kid. A lot of that was obviously due to Alia, but it was also due to the fact that Ron was a wonderful dad. He loved Jada, he really did. He took a lot of pride in his parenting and was just phenomenal in that regard. In an era where you see so many, not just young athletes, but young people shirk that responsibility, he took responsibility for it, he embraced it and he's got just a wonderful daughter. That really fulfilled me as a coach, to see him be such a great dad."

The Badgers' focus was on Iowa. Wisconsin was still looking for its first win over the Hawkeyes since 1976 and had gone 0-17-1 during that stretch. ESPN and 79, 864 fans, the third-largest crowd in Camp Randall Stadium history, were on hand. The Badgers had been blown out by Syracuse, the only nationally-ranked team they had played thus far in 1997, so the 12th-ranked Hawkeyes presented an opportunity for Wisconsin to prove its worth to the college football world and remain in contention for the conference title. And that's just what the Badgers did, though not in a manner anyone expected. Dayne, the No. 2 rusher in the nation entering the game, was carted off the field after injuring his ankle early in the first quarter, gaining just 24 yards on seven attempts. He did not return. The Badgers turned the ball over three times and accumulated just 225 yards of total offense. But a stout defensive effort limited Iowa – which was averaging 43.6 points per game at the time – to 10 points, and Dayne's backup, Eddie Faulkner, rushed for 119 yards and Wisconsin's only touchdown to lead the Badgers to victory. Though two of the nation's best teams – No. 1 Michigan and No. 6 Penn State – remained on the regular-season docket, the Badgers were still in the hunt. But only for a short time.

Dayne missed the next week's game against the Wolverines as his ankle healed, and despite an inspired 102-yard rushing effort from Carl McCullough (who hadn't played in five games) in his final home appearance, the Badgers dropped a 26-16 decision. One week later they fell flat at Penn State and lost 35-10. Wisconsin would be heading to Tampa for a January 1 date with 11th-ranked Georgia in the Outback Bowl.

Wisconsin's 1997 season ended much like it began. Georgia was loaded with stars like Hines Ward and Robert Edwards, and the Bulldogs, led by quarterback Mike Bobo's 26-of-28 passing performance, rolled over the Badgers 33-6. Dayne was held to 36 yards on 14 carries. Like Syracuse, the Bulldogs were one of the best teams Wisconsin faced during the Alvarez era.

The 1997 season was not a bad one for Dayne or the Badgers. The sophomore tailback missed 12 quarters of action and still finished fifth nationally with a 142.0 yards-per-game rushing average. He became the first sophomore to be a finalist for the Doak Walker Award, given to the nation's top running back. *The Football News* tabbed him as a first-team All-American and *Madison* Magazine named him its sports personality of the year in a vote by the city's residents. He rushed for 1,457 yards and 15 touchdowns on 263 attempts, each a statistic that ranked fourth in school history. Dayne accomplished all of this while battling nagging shoulder, groin, ankle and knee ailments throughout the season. The Badgers' 8-5 record was respectable, but ultimately dissatisfying considering they were 8-2 with two regular season contests and a bowl game remaining. That sense of dissatisfaction, however, proved to be a silver lining because it helped to fuel the greatest two-year run in school history.

Barry Alvarez normally called his team together in the McClain Auditorium at Camp Randall Stadium early in the spring semester for something of a "state of the union" meeting. The goal was to re-cap the previous season, address academics and winter conditioning and look ahead to spring practice. Preparing to leave toward the end of the 1998 meeting, Alvarez asked his players if anyone had anything to say.

"I had given it some thought, but wasn't really comfortable in front of a group like that and I didn't want to separate myself from my peers or teammates and be that guy up front," said McIntosh, now halfway through his career as a Badger. "But I thought it was worthwhile and the point I made was that I had kind of taken inventory of where we'd come from the season before. We'd gotten to the Outback Bowl and Georgia just killed us, just humiliated us. I just kind of took a survey of how many guys had a good time down there and what they thought of the game and the season. In my mind I'm thinking we've got this running back who, in hindsight – I don't think I'm out of line with this – after that Georgia game I think flirted with the idea of coming out into the NFL. He obviously had the potential to do that. We had five returning starters on the O-line and some skill players who were unbelievable. We had all the tools. Basically, the point I made was that if there was ever a time to take the next step and look around and take inventory of what we had ... we had everything we needed sitting right there. I said 'I didn't come here to play in the Outback Bowl; I came here to play in the Rose Bowl.' There's truth in that."

McIntosh had come to Madison on the heels of the 1994 Rose Bowl win. He was a native of Wisconsin, and he had been inspired and excited to see how the entire state had rallied around offensive lineman and Brookfield, Wisconsin, native Joe Panos and the rest of the Badgers at that time. But the Badgers had gone 20-15-2 during McIntosh's three years (including his redshirt year in 1995) in Madison. It was not what he had envisioned when he signed to play at Wisconsin.

"We'd gone a few years in kind of a decline," McIntosh said. "We weren't heading in the direction that we'd hoped. My point was to make people aware of what I thought our expectation should be. And it worked – through winter conditioning and spring practice and even at camp at the seminary, in the workouts in summertime. Everybody would call it up at the end [of practice or workouts]. The Rose Bowl was the common chant at the end. We would close out everything with the Rose Bowl. It reminded everybody what we were trying to accomplish.

"Actually, I remember Barry prohibiting us from doing that at camp [in 1998]. He told us we hadn't earned the right to do so. But every year at camp we'd sit down with Barry and come up with the team goals. It wasn't hard that year; we'd kind of made that vow the January before, seven months earlier. So that was the goal. Selfishly, I wanted a piece of that. I didn't want to be part of the program that let down on the expectation."

Though he was not a vocal leader, McIntosh had become a leader nonetheless.

"I really bought into Barry's philosophy: eliminate distractions, concentrate on what you can control, put your nose to the grindstone and keep working," McIntosh said. "Work hard, work hard, work hard day after day. I never read the papers (in Madison). I kind of lived in this bubble there for five years. It was kind of nice, actually. Just worry about what you can control. I was fortunate enough to be the captain of [both the 1998 and 1999] teams. By that time, I had two years of starts under my belt and I kind of felt like the old man having traveled my freshman year, so I didn't have a hard time with [the leadership role]. I guess I earned the right."

Running backs coach Brian White clearly remembers McIntosh's tide-turning statement to his teammates in January of 1998.

"I was in that meeting kind of half listening to a lot of things," White said. "Then all of a sudden – boom! – that grabbed my attention. It jarred me. At first I thought he was absolutely hallucinogenic to think that we could get thrashed by Georgia and all of a sudden we're going to go win the Big Ten championship and play in the Rose Bowl. But that really set the table for how that team worked. The leadership was incredible both offensively and defensively. I've never been around a football team that had more legitimate leaders with great core values that handled all the issues and problems that, inevitably, every football team has. He solved it. Plus they had great personality. They knew how to have a good time, but they also knew when it was time to work. They knew where the line was. And Mac was really the leader on that football team. They were always watching film together; they were always doing more and doing the extra that gives you a chance to win.

"And [offensive line coach Jim Hueber] always did a great job of cultivating toughness and tenacity," White continued. "We were going to be the most physical team in the Big Ten and our players believed that. Our offensive linemen believed that the reason why we won at Wisconsin was because of them, because they were more physical than anybody in the Big Ten. They were going to beat any team we played, whether it would be Michigan, Ohio State, Penn State, we could out-tough them. That was the philosophy of Barry's and they bought into it and they really fashioned themselves as tough guys. And Mac was there. He was the conductor of the orchestra, so to speak, the band leader. It was really something special to be part of and see that whole season and see everything unfold and watch the way they worked and put it all together."

It was not just physical toughness, however, that characterized the Badgers' championship teams of the late 1990s. There was something else, a collective chip on the shoulders of many of the players for one reason or another. For McIntosh it was getting the program back to the level he felt it belonged. Cecil Martin felt the same way.

"The '94 Rose Bowl team did something special in really building the program and then we didn't go to a bowl (in 1995)," Martin said. "We ended up in the Copper Bowl in 1996, which was okay, but it wasn't a January 1st bowl. Then we ended up back down in Tampa for the Outback Bowl. That season we lost some games we shouldn't have lost. We were a good team that year. So coming into [the 1998] training camp we had a chip on our shoulder from that loss to Georgia. That's when we set that goal to go to the Rose Bowl and win. I think the chip on our shoulder was all-encompassing from the '94 Rose Bowl to the struggles of not going to a bowl and then gradually working our way up and feeling like there was only one goal we wanted. We had some serious, serious leaders and efforts that I hadn't seen since my freshman year. Guys really bought in and hit it hard. I remember once we went and saw John Dettmann on a Saturday morning. Our summer workouts were already tough enough, but we were so committed. [Dettmann] said, 'If you want it, come on.' So we all showed up at his house on a Saturday morning asking for more work. Ron was right there with us. And we were running hills near Dettmann's house. That was the kind of chip on our shoulder we had. It was from the past."

Dettmann, who in his role spent as much time with the players as anyone in the program, recalls the tenacity and desire to prove something that was such a huge part of the Badger football program at the time.

"Some of the guys from those teams … Donnel Thompson grew up selling Cokes in the stands," Dettmann said. "I think there was a little chip on the shoulder. I think there was a closeness with that group, a work ethic, a toughness. There was a great leadership quality to a lot of those kids. The McIntoshes, the Ghidorzis, the Thompsons, the Doerings. You could make a pretty long list. We didn't have just one or two. We had a whole slew of them."

For some of the players in the program, those born and raised in Wisconsin, there was a tremendous sense of pride in representing the flagship school in their home state. Some of those players – defensive back/linebacker Bob Adamov and defensive back Jason Doering to name a couple – were walk-ons who went on to start and star on two Big Ten and Rose Bowl championship teams.

"We had a great core of Wisconsin athletes when we were there," said linebacker Chris Ghidorzi. "McIntosh, Doering, Adamov, Thompson, just to name a few. It was one of those things where guys took huge pride in having a successful Wisconsin team. I think Barry's on record saying his best teams were when he had great athletes from Wisconsin. The pride in winning at Wisconsin, that's why we went there. Chris McIntosh stood up in one of our meetings and said 'I didn't come to Wisconsin to go to the Outback Bowl, I came to Wisconsin to go to the Rose Bowl.' That kind of set the tone for what it meant to have pride in Wisconsin and what we were about and how we were going to carry ourselves and go about our business in working to get to that goal."

Still others, like Ferrario and Thompson, were fueled not just by team goals but personal ones, too. Ferrario had been spurned by Penn State. Recruiters had backed off Thompson after he was injured as a high school senior.

"I had a chip on my shoulder from day one," Thompson said. "I certainly felt I could have been a scholarship player for many of the universities in the Big Ten, but a lot of them turned their backs and pretty much stopped calling me, so I certainly had something to prove. I had something to prove to my teammates that I could contribute to the team and be a major contributor. But after that I wanted to prove something to a lot of those coaches who passed me over, said I was too short or had an injured arm or didn't recruit in Wisconsin. As a team, I definitely think so. If you remember back to our first Rose Bowl, Craig James called us the worst Rose Bowl team ever. I don't know how many guys from that team went to the NFL. The audacity to call us the worst Rose Bowl team ever; those types of things were always consistent slaps in the face. And I think it fueled us as a team, definitely."

Alvarez was never afraid to challenge his teams to try to accomplish something that those outside the program thought unlikely or impossible. His ability to communicate that to his players, combined with the hunger that had developed among the players in the program at the time, produced something very potent. Alvarez was expertly pushing and prodding a group that, looking back, really didn't need much extra motivation. The Badgers were hungry and they bought what Alvarez was selling, no questions asked.

"[Alvarez] instilled that whole notion that the world was against us, they didn't think we were good enough, but that as long as we believed in ourselves and got after it, we could [achieve our goals]," Martin said. "But coach had that swagger about him and he passed that swagger on to us. He let us believe that we could walk with a swagger and you walk with a swagger by winning and winning the right way and doing the right things in order to win. I do remember that. Stick your chest out. You've worked hard. Go after it and go get it. That was a theme that he brought here and I think it was the right thing because of where the program was when he first got here. And just because the program has risen up doesn't mean you abandon what got you here."

CHAPTER SIX
The Road to the Roses

All of the character, desire, commitment and talent in the Wisconsin football program was a year older heading into the 1998 season. In fact, the Badgers were returning 19 starters, plus their kicker and punter, from the 1997 team, and those who put together preseason polls took notice. Wisconsin was ranked 20th (its highest preseason ranking since 1994) in both the coaches and Associated Press polls prior to the start of the 1998 campaign. Expectations were high not only within the program, but outside as well. What was missing from the previous summer, however, was the white-hot spotlight that had focused on Dayne following his otherworldly freshman season. There were no Great Dane photo shoots in the summer of 1998 and there was no build-up to a huge game played just outside New York City like there was for the 1997 opener against Syracuse. Dayne had rushed for 3,320 regular-season yards (the NCAA did not count statistics from bowl games in those years) in his first two seasons, a figure that was well over halfway to the NCAA Division I record of 6,082 set by Pittsburgh's Tony Dorsett from 1973-76. Dayne made his share of preseason All-America teams and was named the Big Ten preseason offensive player of the year. And he was, of course, mentioned among the 1998 Heisman Trophy candidates along with players like Texas running back Ricky Williams and quarterbacks Tim Couch of Kentucky and Cade McNown of UCLA. But the frenzy from the summer of 1997 had eased.

"We haven't put the big hype on him this year because it's not necessary," Alvarez told reporters as the 1998 season approached. "People know who he is and his productivity will determine how well he'll do with all the awards at the end of the year. That's just how he likes it. He just likes to go out and play."

Dayne would not, however, play in the season opener at San Diego State. He had sprained his ankle during fall camp and was held out of action as the Badgers took on the Aztecs. Backup Eddie Faulkner left the game with a shoulder injury in the first quarter. For a team that hung its hat on a strong running game, it was not the ideal start to the season. But redshirt freshman Carlos Daniels, the third-string running back, filled in ably for Dayne and Faulkner, carrying 28 times for 113 yards, including 62 in the fourth quarter as the Badgers held on for a 26-14 victory at Qualcomm Stadium. The teams were tied 7-7 at the half and Wisconsin trailed 14-13 early in the fourth quarter before Mike Samuel turned a quarterback draw into a 47-yard touchdown run to account for the winning points with 11:56 left to play. McIntosh broke his right thumb in the second quarter, but let team doctors know in no uncertain terms that he was not coming out of the game. A cast was put on the thumb at halftime and McIntosh finished the game. It was emblematic of the toughness, leadership skills and determination on that team. By the end of his career, McIntosh would start 50 consecutive games.

The Badger offensive line had begun to mature. Costa, Ferrario and Rabach had a year under their belts as starters. McIntosh had become the clear leader of the group. And right tackle Aaron Gibson, 6-foot-7 and 378 pounds, had developed into not only a college football novelty of sorts – he had been featured in the *New York Times Magazine* and on ABC's 20/20 – but a standout player who was a preseason first-team All-American. Gibson wrote poetry, enjoyed fishing and could both dunk a basketball and do the splits. He had a friendly, outgoing personality, prompting Wisconsin sports information director Steve Malchow to call him "one of the kindest athletes I ever got a chance to work with." But it was Gibson's combination of size, strength and athletic ability on the football field that brought the national media to Madison. Gibson had been a blocking tight end in 1996 before starting 10 games at right tackle as a junior. He wore size 19 shoes and a size 62 jacket, and he had a 47 ½ inch waist. Riddell, the equipment maker, had never produced a larger helmet than Gibson's.

The potential stumbling block at San Diego State was out of the way, and Dayne was ready to return to the lineup the following week in the home-opener against Ohio. The Badgers made quick work of the Bobcats in a 45-0 shutout. A stellar defensive effort, led by defensive end Tom Burke and linebacker Donnel Thompson, limited Ohio to just 102 yards of total offense and Dayne, though not quite 100 percent, rushed for 111 yards and three touchdowns on 20 carries in a little more than 2 ½ quarters. Dayne's perform-ance brought him within 32 yards of Billy Marek's school career rushing record, a mark that would fall a week later.

Marek had starred at Wisconsin in the mid-1970s and was a three-time first-team All-Big Ten selection at the same time that Ohio State's Archie Griffin was winning back-to-back Heisman Trophies and setting the conference record for career rushing yards. Marek became the Badgers' all-time rushing leader after fin-ishing his career in 1975 with 3,709 yards, along with a school-record 44 touchdowns. Among his great feats as a Badger was a stretch during the last three games of the 1974 season when he rushed for a combined 740 yards and 13 touchdowns in wins over Iowa, Northwestern and Minnesota. Marek was on hand at Camp Randall Stadium and recognized at halftime when Dayne and the Badgers played host to UNLV on September 19.

The Rebels jumped out to a 7-0 lead on a 50-yard interception return for a touchdown, but they never scored again. Wisconsin, on the other hand, grabbed a 24-7 halftime lead and cruised to a 52-7 victory. Dayne, who eclipsed Marek's school rushing mark three carries into the game, finished with 108 yards on just 13 attempts. Dayne and Marek appeared together at the post-game news conference in the McClain Center where Marek presented the new record-holder with the game ball. Marek remembers a number of the qualities Dayne brought to the table.

"First off, I think Ron is just a quality guy," says Marek. "Just a nice person. I think he went about his business in a great way. I love the fact that his work ethic came through just the way he ran. It just was very methodical, very strong and he had quick feet. To me it just appeared that he could do everything. He had good speed, he had great quickness in his feet and he had incredible power."

Considering his size, Dayne's athletic abilities were something of a surprise to Marek.

"I was very surprised at how quick he was," Marek said. "If he wanted to, I'm sure he could have run around a lot of people and not caused as much damage to his body. But he had his option. You know, it's one thing to be fast straight ahead; it's another thing to shift your body weight and, with the weight he had, to be able to move as quick as he did was very impressive."

Marek, who still has the same season tickets he secured after he graduated from Wisconsin, is also surprised his rushing record lasted as long as it did.

"There are a few ways to look at it," Marek says of his record's longevity. "Football evolved (after Marek played) into where it was more of a platoon system. Yes, I did alternate with a few other guys during my career, but it's very different than when Ron came through and you had multiple backs in there for different reasons. It wasn't the same when we played. We threw the ball effectively; we just didn't throw it very often. You didn't have the platooning as much as you do now with third down specialists. The flow of the game is very different today. It's much more difficult to hit big numbers when you've got so many people coming and going. Those records sat there a long time because of the platooning and things that happened in the game. So that makes it a little bit different. But that's a long time to be sitting there. It's almost disappointing. We had a few years there that the program wasn't so great and I guess you could look at it and say on one hand it's really nice [the record's] sat there that long, but it was a little disappointing that our teams didn't play better. So when [Dayne] broke the record, I was very pleased for him and the fact that it was a nice event."

Among the characteristics of the Badgers during both the Marek and Dayne eras was quality offensive line play and a chemistry between the line and its tailback. Marek enjoyed running behind top-notch linemen much the same way Dayne did.

"It's a timing issue," Marek said of his relationship with his offensive line. "You have a cohesive group that gets along well together and you've all got the same instincts on what you want to do on the football field. But if you're not seeing eye to eye with everybody on the offensive line as far as what you want to accomplish on the field, that's where you'd have an issue. The guys we had were just outstanding. Terry Stieve, Dennis Lick, Joe Norwick – Mike Webster was there our sophomore year – John Reimer, all those guys were big, tough guys, guys who really took me under their wing and basically said, 'We're going to get you those thousand yards.' Where I was trying to get through the hole and go as far as I could, I think these guys had it more in their minds that they're going to be successful and make sure that their running back hits 1,000 yards every year. I think it was important to them as much as anybody. During that time, there wasn't a lot of passing. That's just the way the game was played. Gregg Bohlig was very effective as a quarterback, but the game plan just wasn't to throw that often. So defenses kind of sat on us. And it was even that much harder to run the ball, but those guys were very determined. Just a great, tough group of guys."

Marek could just as easily have been talking about the linemen who blocked for Dayne.

The lopsided win over UNLV left the Badgers ranked 14th nationally with their first 3-0 mark since 1996. They hadn't been 4-0 since the magical 1993 Rose Bowl season. Northwestern, whom Wisconsin had battled down to the wire in each of their previous two meetings, came to Camp Randall Stadium for Round 3 on September 26. It turned into a knockout for the Badgers. A 46-yard touchdown run highlighted a season-high 168-yard effort by Dayne, and the Wisconsin defense continued its suffocating play in a 38-7 win over the Wildcats. The Badgers then left Bloomington the following Saturday with a 24-20 victory over Indiana. Dayne gained 130 yards against the Hoosiers to tie Marshall Faulk as the second-fastest player ever to pass the 4,000-yard mark. He also moved into ninth place on the Big Ten career rushing list. Wisconsin was 5-0 overall, 2-0 in the Big Ten and ranked 12th in the nation with Purdue and its pass-happy quarterback, Drew Brees, coming to town for a Homecoming contest that would be just the third night game in Camp Randall Stadium history. Wisconsin entered the game ranked No. 5 nationally in total defense and would need a complete effort to handle Brees, who had thrown for a school-record 522 yards and six touchdowns in just three quarters in a 56-21 win over Minnesota a week earlier.

Samuel put the Badgers ahead 14-3 after the first quarter thanks to a pair of touchdown runs, but the Boilermakers pulled even for a 17-17 deadlock at halftime. In the first half Brees completed 24 of 36 passes for 206 yards. Late in the third quarter freshman cornerback Jamar Fletcher jumped on a Brees pass and returned it 52 yards for a touchdown and a 24-17 Wisconsin lead. Dayne, on the way to a 33-carry, 127-yard performance, added the eventual game-winning points with a 1-yard touchdown run midway through the final quarter. Purdue scored late, but the Badgers recovered an onside kick to secure the win. Brees set an NCAA record with 83 passing attempts and tied the national standard with 55 completions. He threw for 494 yards, but the Badgers intercepted him four times. Wisconsin had survived the unprecedented aerial show, remained undefeated at 6-0 and moved up to No. 9 in the Associated Press poll.

The victory over the Boilermakers will always be remembered by Badger fans for Brees' performance and Fletcher's interception return for a third-quarter touchdown. What many don't know is that at the conclusion of that third quarter, a Wisconsin football tradition – "Jump Around" – was born. That season had seen the debut of the "student section race," a competition run on the stadium scoreboard between the letters of the student seating sections at Camp Randall Stadium. The UW athletics marketing staff normally played music following the race and that night they chose "Jump Around" by a band called House of Pain. Seeing that fans were enthusiastically doing just as the song commanded, it became a staple at Badger homes games.

Wisconsin followed up the Purdue win with three consecutive lopsided victories: 37-3 at Illinois, 31-0 at Iowa and 26-7 at home over Minnesota. It was a stretch during which Dayne saw his heaviest workload of the season, rushing for a combined 487 yards and five touchdowns on 113 attempts. He ran all over Illinois, notching 190 yards and three scores for a total of 686 yards and nine touchdowns in three games against the Fighting Illini. In that game he also reached 45 career touchdowns, surpassing Marek's school record of 44. He had become the Big Ten's fifth-leading career rusher halfway through this junior year. Fullback Cecil Martin, noting Dayne's humility, told reporters after the win over Illinois that, "In the locker room a little while ago, [McIntosh] asked him how many yards he had and Ron said, '*We* had 190.' That's how he is. Ron's not only a good football player, he's a special person."

The eighth-ranked Badgers were 9-0 for the first time since 1901 as they headed into a November 14 matchup at No. 15 Michigan. Wisconsin entered the game leading the nation in run defense, giving up an average of 63 yards per game. The Badgers ranked third in scoring defense (9.1 points a game) and fourth in total defense (249 yards allowed a game) and had held their last three opponents to a combined 10 points. Dayne had run for at least 108 yards in eight straight games. Some in the media, however, questioned the Badgers' gaudy statistics, claiming they had been compiled against subpar opposition. Wisconsin took the field at Michigan Stadium and proceeded to lend credence to the critics' voices. The Badgers jumped out to a 7-0 lead, but Michigan responded and went on to a 27-10 victory. The Wolverines not only punctured the Badger defense, accumulating 476 yards of total offense, but they shut down Dayne by limiting him to just 53 yards on 16 carries. Wisconsin's perfect record had been blemished and now the Badgers would need to defeat 14th-ranked Penn State at home and hope for an Ohio State victory over Michigan that would result in a three-way deadlock for the Big Ten championship and give Wisconsin the tie-breaker and a trip to Pasadena for the Rose Bowl.

Coach John Cooper's Ohio State Buckeyes already had things well in hand in Columbus – they led Michigan 31-16 late in the fourth quarter – when Penn State's Travis Forney kicked off to get things rolling at Camp Randall Stadium. Just past the midway point of the first quarter, Dayne was injured as he was tackled after a carry along the Wisconsin sideline. He left the field, but later returned and ended up grinding out 95 yards on 23 attempts. As Dayne was exiting the playing field, stadium public address announcer Mike Mahnke told the Badgers and their fans what they wanted to hear. The final from Columbus was Ohio State 31, Michigan 16. Now, it was clear. A Wisconsin win over

the Nittany Lions would give McIntosh and his fellow captains –
who had gone to Alvarez late in the summer to emphasize their
goal of winning the Big Ten and going to the Rose Bowl – the
chance they had been dreaming about.

Freshman Nick Davis actually accounted for all the points the
Badgers would need, electrifying the crowd with an 82-yard punt
return for a touchdown with 26 seconds left in the first quarter. It
was the second punt the speedy Davis had brought back for a score
in 1998. When Alvarez asked Davis before the season whether or
not he could field punts, Davis famously said, "Coach, I can catch a
B.B. in the dark." He was true to his word.

Wide receiver Chris Chambers made a terrific touchdown catch
early in the second quarter and Matt Davenport added a field goal
for a 17-0 halftime lead. The stingy Badger defense, led by All-
American defensive end Tom Burke, was back to its old self and
limited the Nittany Lions to just three points in a 24-3 Wisconsin
victory. The old scoreboard that hung on the outside of the north
wall of the UW Field House said it all: "ROSE BOWL HERE WE
COME!!!!!!" and "SEE YOU IN PASADENA."

The Badgers, many of them with their helmets in one hand and
roses in the other, ran off the field and into their locker room on
the ground floor of the McClain Center. Alvarez addressed them
as a group:

"You learned a lesson in life," he told his players. "The first day
of camp, Mac and Bobby (Adamov) said, 'Coach, we didn't come
here just to go to bowl games; we want to go to the Rose Bowl.'
Enough said. If everybody believes and everybody understands the
goal and the mission, and stays focused, and everybody gets on the
same page to achieve that goal, nobody can stop you and that's
exactly what happened! I've never been as proud of a football team,
a coaching staff … guys playing off their strengths, not trying to
do something you can't do, and taking pride in who you are. You're
champions. Be proud of it. Carry yourselves like champions."

Alvarez then added, "Actually, there were two goals. Go to the Rose Bowl. And win the Rose Bowl!"

As Alvarez called the players up, however, his attention was drawn away to Director of Athletics Pat Richter, who had with him Robert Vowels, an assistant commissioner with the Big Ten Conference. Vowels stepped forward as the players took a knee and presented the Badgers with the conference championship trophy. No pomp and circumstance. No microphone. Nothing fancy. It was an impromptu moment, but the understated, no-frills presentation perfectly fit the workmanlike, no-frills Badgers. Martin, one-fourth of an extraordinary group of team captains that season, took hold of the trophy and spoke to his teammates.

"Fellas, we all had a part in this, baby," Martin said. "Everybody in this locker room had a part in this. Coaches, players, support staff. Everybody had a part in this. Hey, baby, we're champions!"

They were champions, but they clearly had not earned the universal respect of the college football world. Prior to the Rose Bowl, CBS analyst Craig James called Wisconsin "the worst team I can remember playing in the Rose Bowl." And UCLA, whom the Badgers would face in Pasadena, had come one late-season loss to Miami from playing for the national championship. The Bruins' consolation prize was a New Year's Day date with a team some thought did not belong on the same field with them. The two teams were polar opposites. Wisconsin was 89th nationally in total offense, relying primarily on the running of Dayne and Samuel – behind an ever-improving offensive line – to control the ball and grind down opposing defenses. Even less sexy were the Badgers' defense (No. 1 nationally in points allowed and No. 5 in total defense) and special teams units (third in the country in net punting and ninth in punt returns). UW also led the nation in turnover margin. The Bruins, on the other hand, were the nation's fifth highest-scoring team and were eighth in total offense. They averaged 40.5 points per game to Wisconsin's 31.3. It was defensively where there was a major disparity. UCLA was allowing 27.5 points per game and ranked 70th nationally in run defense and 99th in total defense. If the Badgers could slow down quarterback Cade McNown and the UCLA offense, Dayne and Samuel might be able to run up and down the field all afternoon.

Ten days before the Rose Bowl, Dayne announced at a news conference at the Kohl Center that he would be returning to Wisconsin for his senior year.

"Some of my reasons I thought this was the best decision for me were my teammates, the coaches and I also wanted to improve as a football player," Dayne said that day. "I have a daughter out here, and I'd like to stay with her for another year and get closer with her and her mother."

Dayne also had something to prove to NFL draft analysts and scouts, who were now saying he would likely not be a first-round pick in the 1999 draft. And, of course, Dayne's return gave him a shot at breaking the NCAA Division I career rushing record recently set by Texas' Ricky Williams, as well as winning the 1999 Heisman Trophy.

"One of the things about Ronnie, I think he listens to people," said Rob Reid, Dayne's uncle and legal guardian when Dayne was a teenager. "I believe Coach Alvarez and (assistant coach) Bernie (Wyatt) really gave him a good assessment about what he could do if he stayed another year and how that would enhance his value about where he would go in the draft. It may have been a tough decision for him, but Ronnie listens to people that he respects and who really care about him. So that may have outweighed the natural inclination for most kids to say, 'You know what, I'm getting out of here and I'm going to make the money.' So he did a great job, I think, of just trusting the people around him."

Returning to Wisconsin would give Dayne a chance to answer the doubters and critics. Proving people wrong and accomplishing the unexpected was something he had been doing his entire life.

"I was at my sister's house and my sister had a little boy and my other sister had a little boy," said Dayne's mother, Brenda. "They were on the floor playing with this Nerf football. And they were just throwing it back to each other – knocking it back to each other and everything. Ronnie threw the ball to his cousin D.J., threw it over his head and D.J. turned around, looking to get it. I was sitting there talking to my sisters. We were laughing and talking and Ronnie got up and ran across the floor and picked up the football and came back and all of us were looking at him. And my sister said, 'You didn't tell me he could walk.' And I said, 'I didn't know he could walk!' He ran over and got the football and ran back and sat down. He was seven months old. All my family will tell you that because they were in shock."

Dayne, full of energy, was always bigger than other kids his age. In fact, his mother even carried around a miniature birth certificate just in case she had to prove her son's age to someone. When Dayne was 3 ½ years old he had a friend twice his age who played organized football after school in Lynchburg, Virginia, where Dayne and his family lived at the time. Young Ron would stand off to the side playing with his own ball while the older boys played on the field. One day the coach approached Brenda and asked her why Ron wasn't playing.

"At that time they went by age – he had to be in kindergarten," Brenda said. "But they didn't ask me how old he was because he was the same size as the other kids. So I let him go. Every day he'd go to his little nursery school, I'd pick him up and he'd come home. When it was time for football practice, I'd take him down there and they'd ask him, 'Ronnie, how was school – you doing good?' He'd say, 'Yeah.' They'd ask, 'Do you like your teachers?' And he'd say, 'Yeah.' They didn't know he was going to nursery school at the time! When he turned 4, that's when they asked me his age. I said he was 4 and the coach was like, 'You mean he's been playing here?' I said, 'You never asked me for his birth certificate or anything.' I just wanted him to have something to do that took all that energy because he was driving me crazy! So they let him play."

Brenda also recalled the first time Dayne started carrying the football.

"The second year he played, they had him playing defense. They had him tackling people. After every play, Ronnie would be out on the ground laughing and talking with the guys he tackled. So the coach would come over and say something to him. One time he grabbed him by the arm, so I walked to him and I said, 'Listen, let me tell you something. That one right there, he belongs to me – don't put your hands on him. What you have to do is give him something to do. Give him the football, okay? Put the football in his hands and you don't have to worry about him talking.' They laughed at me and I said, 'No, I'm serious. If you holler at him again, he's not playing.' They put him in there, they gave him the football and that's how he started running with the football. He played in a Toys for Tots game and I was a little late for the beginning of the game, and as I'm running in, I see him running towards me, it was like he was piggy-backing. They had kicked the ball off and Ronnie got the ball and he started running. His little friend was on the other team and he jumped on Ronnie's back and Ronnie carried him all the way down for the touchdown. They laughed about it, but it was okay."

It was okay when her son laughed, but Brenda also found others laughing at young Ron. She responded with quiet confidence because she knew her young boy was a special athlete.

"Ronnie was still big and he was the last leg of this 4x100 relay, and when they came out on the field, the people in the stands started laughing," Brenda remembers. "They were laughing at him. I was just sitting there. I didn't say anything because I knew how fast he was. Three of his cousins ran the first three legs and when they gave that baton to Ronnie, he came across the finish line and it was complete silence besides me screaming and hollering. I remember one lady said to me, 'You must be his mother.' And I said, 'Yeah.' She said, 'That's why you never said a word.' And I replied, 'I don't have to. I just let him do his thing.'"

Dayne's 1998 season, like the one before it, was a success by most measuring sticks. He was a first-team Walter Camp All-American, a Doak Walker Award finalist and a consensus first-team All-Big Ten selection after becoming the first player since Michigan State's Lorenzo White (1985 and 1987) to lead the conference in rushing twice. He had become Wisconsin's career rushing leader. He was just 744 yards behind Big Ten legend and career rushing leader Archie Griffin of Ohio State. And he would enter the 1999 campaign needing 1,717 yards to break Ricky Williams' NCAA Division I mark, set the previous year. Dayne had done all of this, but still faced critics who questioned his speed or durability or perceived lack of production against quality opponents. He was, however, about to silence his doubters with a superlative performance in Pasadena. Much like his mother at his youth track meet, Dayne didn't need to say anything. He would just do his thing. And so would the rest of the Badgers.

Few gave the Badgers a chance to win the last Rose Bowl of the 20th century, and few thought Wisconsin and UCLA made for much of a matchup. They were wrong on both counts. The 1999 Rose Bowl – the first-ever Bowl Championship Series (BCS) game – was one of the most entertaining contests in that storied bowl's history. Dayne got the scoring started with a 54-yard touchdown run late in the first quarter thanks to a hole created by Ferrario and McIntosh. UCLA struck right back, however, when McNown hit Jermaine Lewis with a 38-yard scoring pass. And that's the way the game went, back and forth. On the Badgers' ensuing possession, Samuel set up Dayne's seven-yard touchdown run with a 52-yard sprint down the field in front of the Wisconsin sideline. UCLA responded immediately when Freddie Mitchell connected with Durell Price for a 61-yard touchdown pass. McNown threw a 41-yard touchdown pass to Danny Farmer five minutes later and the Bruins led 21-14. Dayne picked up his third touchdown run from 10 yards out with three minutes left in the second quarter, and Davenport booted a 40-yard field goal with 17 seconds left in the half for a 24-21 lead that the Badgers never relinquished. The furious scoring pace featured drives of 75, 80, 85, 65, 90, 80 and 56 yards, though just two of those drives were more than three minutes in length. Dayne hammered away at the Bruins for 173 yards and three scores on just 15 carries in the first half as the Badgers took a 258-54 edge in rushing yards. UCLA did just the opposite through the air, throwing for 251 yards to Wisconsin's 75.

Dayne's 22-yard touchdown run – his Rose Bowl record-tying fourth of the game – put the Badgers ahead, 31-21, with 11:28 left in the third quarter. Dayne showed his remarkable vision and cut-back ability on the play as he started outside to the right before cutting back inside and leaving Bruin cornerback Marques Anderson grasping at air. Lewis' 10-yard run later in the quarter brought the Bruins to within 31-28, but Fletcher's 46-yard interception return for a touchdown with 14:08 left in the fourth quarter gave the Badgers a 38-28 advantage. They held on to win 38-31. Their mission as a team was complete. They set a school record for wins in a season with 11 and they silenced their remaining critics. They had beaten UCLA in a shootout, but they had done it their way. Dayne was named the game MVP after rushing for 246 yards and four touchdowns on only 27 carries, a 9.1 yards-per-attempt average. He had shown durability, toughness (his shoulder injury from the Penn State game was not 100 percent), vision, speed and power.

"Take away Ron Dayne and we win the game," UCLA offensive lineman Kris Farris said after the game. "He's the best in the nation."

Farris's teammate, linebacker Tony White, put it another way. "He can overpower you," White said of Dayne. "But then when you think he's going to overpower you, he uses his finesse and makes you miss. I don't think we've seen a running back like that all year."

It was one of the most satisfying wins of Alvarez's career.

"That was just fun to watch because that team was supposed to play in the national championship game," Alvarez said of UCLA. "That was a very talented UCLA team and no one had really stopped or slowed down their offense, and we didn't slow them down for a while. That was a slugfest. But there again, they couldn't tackle Ron. It was just one of those days when you know the guy's in a groove. You hand him the ball and it's like everyone else is standing still, and he hesitates and, "pshooo," he's into the secondary. They were taking bad angles and, again, they didn't look like they wanted to tackle him."

Dayne's scintillating performance against UCLA made him an immediate front-runner for the 1999 Heisman Trophy, along with Florida State wide receiver Peter Warrick, Purdue quarterback Drew Brees and a host of others. Alvarez's approach with his team was simple and straightforward: with team success will come individual success.

CHAPTER SEVEN
Run For the Record

Barry Alvarez's message to his defending Big Ten champions before the 1999 season started emphasized how critical
each and every player's role would be in assuring the success of
not only the team, but Ron Dayne as well.

"I always talked about everyone's role on that team and how
important it was and everybody had to accept it," Alvarez said.
"That year we had a chance to accomplish some special things. Ron
had a chance to be the all-time leading rusher in college football. I
pointed to the offensive line and said, 'No one ever gives you any
attention. No one ever pays any attention to the offensive line, no
one ever gives you any credit – except when you give up a sack.
But if you block for somebody that ran for more yards than anybody in the history of college football, man, you've got something
to be proud of. You can always hang your hat on that and talk
about that for the rest of your life.' Ronnie had a chance to win the
Heisman Trophy. But for him to win the Heisman Trophy, we had
to win a lot of games. And that meant every one of them could
contribute in this. Scout squad guys had to do a good job of
preparing the guys, the starters. Special teams had to step up.
Everybody had to produce, everybody had to contribute something.
I told them, 'If we win a lot of games and Ronnie has the type of
year that he could have, you all have a piece of it – you all have a
piece of the action."

Alvarez's approach synched well with his veteran players. They
had seen what a team-first philosophy could do and they bought in

to what their coach was selling. They realized, however, that 1999 was a different season than the previous one. Wisconsin was the hunted, not the hunter.

"I certainly think there were expectations and, as a team, you have to have certain expectations for yourself," said Donnel Thompson. "Our goal, always, every year at the University of Wisconsin was to go to the Rose Bowl and that's what it was that year. I thought Coach Alvarez did a fantastic job. He set the Heisman up as a team award. He knew that if Ron Dayne won the Heisman that meant we were winning as a team, [Ron] was running the ball very well, the offensive line was running the ball very well, we were passing the ball very efficiently and, probably on defense, we had to get off the field so we could get the ball back to the offense, relatively quickly. So he set it up as a team goal and he announced it to the team in training camp, I believe. That way it wasn't a Ron thing or an offensive line thing. It was a University of Wisconsin thing. That was very smart of him."

McIntosh agreed, noting the expectation level had changed considerably from the prior year.

"We knew that the way we were going to win games was to give Ron the ball and successfully run the ball and everything would work out from that," McIntosh said. "They were talking about the rushing record. There was the Heisman talk and by that time, personally, there were some pretty serious expectations with my own play and putting together great games to try to boost your draft status – that's the last year. And not to mention coming off the Rose Bowl win, there were some really high expectations, and a lot of pressure that year. It was fun, don't get me wrong. But the '98 season was fun because no one expected us to do what we did. We were the underdog in a lot of games. The '99 season was fun, but we didn't sneak up on anybody. We start-ed 2-2, we were trying to get Ron, in the back of our minds, we were trying to get him the record and trying to win games and through all that, personally, trying to do whatever I can to boost my draft status and everything else. There was just a lot of pressure that year. But it was fun at the same time. It was just a much different year."

The team-first approach notwithstanding, the Heisman Trophy and the NCAA rushing record are still assigned to just one person. There is no question that Alvarez's approach was the right one as far as keeping his entire team focused, but only one man can win the Heisman Trophy and only one can be the all-time rushing leader. That is where sports information director Steve Malchow figured prominently into the equation. He had become someone Dayne trusted, and he would play a signficant role in handling whatever off-the-field attention came Dayne's way.

"More important than anything to Coach Alvarez was that I didn't let any campaign get in the way of our team having success," Malchow said. "First, I was pretty nervous about what I could do that Ron would be comfortable with and, secondly, it had to be something that wouldn't upset the balance on our team. And it had to be legit and fit Ron. I brainstormed all the things I could think of to do that would promote him. I talked to Coach Alvarez about the list and said 'This is a list, A-to-Z, of the types of things I think we can do.' Barry asked me what I thought we ought to do. I picked out a couple things that I thought fit.

"I had noted that Ricky Williams had broken Tony Dorsett's rushing record to become college football's career rushing leader and ended up winning the Heisman Trophy. The more I thought about it, historically, the game of football had been a rushing game and if you broke the all-time rushing record and you were college football's all-time greatest rusher, that's like being the all-time home run champion in baseball. There is no better record. I thought that if Ron could break that record, he's all but guaranteed a trip to New York and that was the goal. I told Ron that. I said, 'If we can get you to New York, we've done our job and the team will have won a lot of games. If you win the award, that's icing on the cake.' My focus, at least campaign-wise, ended up being that career rushing record.

"Barry had mentioned to me that when he was at Notre Dame, they had done postcard campaigns for star players. I thought that if we sent out postcards to media, I wasn't sure how well they'd be read but that at least Ron's picture would go by their desks each week. And that would be an imprint and that's what I was looking for. So, collectively, the decision was made that we would count down his march to becoming college football's all-time leading rusher. That's where the 1,717 started and each week we'd send it out and whatever he'd run for the week before, subtract that. There was a series of 12 weeks of cards. We'd put some fun facts on the back and some statistical oddities and other things about Ron. That's how the postcard campaign about Ron got started. I've been asked many times since about Ron's Heisman Trophy-winning season by other schools and how much money we spent on our Heisman campaign and I say 'very little.' The only expenditure we had was the postcards, which is pretty cheap by today's standards."

In addition to the postcards, Reebok, which was then the official apparel supplier for Badger athletics, sponsored two billboards in Madison that featured Dayne. One was on U.S. Highway 12/18, also known as the Beltline; the other hung on the outside of the south wall of the UW Field House. The Field House billboard was designed so that the yardage Dayne needed to catch Williams' rushing record could be updated each week. Reebok had done something similar in Texas a year earlier when Williams was pursuing the rushing record held by Tony Dorsett. The Field House billboard debuted with the number 1,717 on it.

Malchow was fortunate to be working with a different Dayne than the shy teenager he had met at the Holy Name Seminary back in the summer of 1996. Though Dayne was never what could be called outgoing, he clearly was more comfortable talking to the media and carrying himself in public.

"Ron does pretty well with it all – I don't know if I was in his shoes I could be the same way," said McIntosh, who joined Dayne at the 1999 Big Ten Football Media Days in Chicago. "He has changed a lot in the four years that I've known him, and he's changed in a good way. He's definitely more outspoken now than he ever was."

Jay Wilson, a longtime Madison television sports anchor, also noticed a more relaxed and comfortable Dayne when it came to his dealings with the media.

"Ron was always personable, always pleasurable, always a good guy," Wilson said. "But, boy, it was hard to get an answer you could use. In television news you're looking for 15-18 seconds, and we were ending up getting a lot of five and six seconds, so we'd have to string five here, four here, seven here to get our 15-18 seconds. Ron's second year the five seconds turned into eight seconds and the next year turned into 11 seconds and then by the end, we were getting our 15-18 seconds. That's not to say that everyone should be a home run kind of interview, but I give him credit for working at it and trying to improve himself, just like he tried to improve as a football player.

"When he first came to an interview, he was a struggle," Wilson continued. "We'd come back from interviewing Ron and I remember one time one of our guys, Andy Kendeigh, said, 'I think he put 20 words together in one sentence.' And he was so excited that he finally got Ron to say something to some extent. But he became so much of a national figure that he had to do these interviews and he had to develop that, and he worked hard to develop it, not only as a football player, but as a person. He was a much different guy by the time he left than when he came."

Matt Lepay, the longtime radio play-by-play voice of the Badgers, saw another side to the outwardly quiet Dayne when the cameras and tape recorders were off.

"He didn't have a lot to say," Lepay recalled. "It was kind of funny because, when the tape recorder was off and he was just goofing around, he could mess with you a little bit, even with someone like me who he knew, but we didn't hang together. He could mess around. But when the tape recorder was on or the TV cameras were rolling, you could tell that wasn't something that was very comfortable for him. I think he got better, but you could still tell it was something he would rather not do. He fell into the category of someone who tolerated the interview process."

Dayne may have become more comfortable with the media end of things, but that didn't mean it was all smooth sailing, particularly for Malchow, who was charged with coordinating all of the Heisman hoopla. Malchow told Dayne he would try to keep the media interview requirements to a minimum, but that he needed Dayne to meet him halfway when necessary.

"At the start of the season, I decided to have a national teleconference," Malchow said. "I asked Ron to give me 20-30 minutes of his time. I was going to get [reporters] from all over the country on the phone and let them ask some questions and we'd just kind of go around the horn. So I got it all set up, it was five or 10 minutes outside of when it's supposed to start and no Ron. He never showed up. So I'm on the telephone with probably 25 of the nation's foremost college football writers and they have nobody to interview. I was incredibly embarrassed, extremely upset, ready to, I guess, drop-kick the whole thing because I felt like my reputation was undercut and I had nothing to do with it. So I went to Ron's apartment and we had a pretty heated exchange. I said, 'I have worked my whole life to develop a reputation here and you just undercut it and I'm not dealing with that ever again. You can't leave me hanging like that.' And I am extremely pleased to share that I never had one problem the rest of the year. It was a message that had to be delivered to him or I never would have made it through the year, nor would he, but we had an exceptional relationship after that. I remember telling Barry that I couldn't go through this the whole year if I didn't get better cooperation. Barry eventually said, 'You deal with it – it's your deal. You've got to work through it with him, you got to have a relationship.' It ended up being what paved the way for a really fun season for us. I'm glad we kind of got it out of the way in the preseason."

The 1999 Badgers started the season ranked No. 9 in the nation with good reason. They returned 16 starters from the 1998 unit, including seven on offense, eight on defense and punter Kevin Stemke. The losses included key players like Tom Burke, Bob Adamov, Aaron Gibson, Mike Samuel, Eric Grams, Leonard Taylor, Matt Davenport and Cecil Martin. Gibson, Burke and Martin were selected in the 1999 NFL draft, with Martin joining former UW offensive coordinator Brad Childress in Philadelphia. Martin, in fact, enjoys the unique distinction of having blocked as a fullback for two players who won the Heisman Trophy and set the NCAA rushing record. Martin, of course, blocked for Dayne from 1996-98. He also blocked for Ricky Williams in the 1999 Hula Bowl in Honolulu. Martin had considered the fact that Dayne might have a shot at Williams' mark.

"That never entered my mind until I was in training camp and all season with the Eagles because that's when the campaign began and I was like, 'Wow, he's really like the front runner to make it happen,'" Martin said. "When he rushed for 2,000 yards as a freshman I thought that was unbelievable. But when I was with the Eagles it was wild watching the frenzy, the whole campaign.

"But I did think about it because Ricky Williams came out with me and I blocked for him at the Hula Bowl when I was a senior. He played a few series and I got a chance to block for him, so I've gotten a chance to block for two Heisman Trophy winners."

Perhaps the most critical need for a replacement in 1999, however, was at quarterback. The departed Samuel, often criticized by fans and media, had guided the Badgers to a school record-tying 27 victories and his leadership skills, toughness and playmaking abilities were almost beyond measure.

The top two candidates to succeed Samuel were senior Scott Kavanagh, who had backed up Samuel for three years, and red-shirt freshman Brooks Bollinger from Grand Forks, North Dakota. Kavanagh had completed 53 percent of his passes and thrown six touchdowns in 17 appearances throughout his career. Bollinger had enjoyed a solid spring game performance in April and was an excellent athlete with a good arm, but he had never taken a snap in a college game. Alvarez named Kavanagh the starter for the September 4 opener at home against NCAA Division I-AA opponent Murray State.

Three days before the Murray State game, the Scripps Howard News Service's annual poll of Heisman Trophy voters revealed Dayne as the No. 1 choice to win the award. He was followed by Florida State's Peter Warrick, Purdue's Drew Brees, Penn State's LaVar Arrington, Tennessee's Tee Martin and Texas Tech's Ricky Williams. Dayne, who had been kept from much contact in the spring or in fall camp, was set to start the season healthy for the first time since his freshman year in 1996.

Wisconsin's 1999 season opener turned into the mismatch it was expected to be. The Badgers took a 42-7 halftime lead as Dayne scored three touchdowns and gained 135 yards on 20 car-ries. Nick Davis added a 76-yard punt return for a touchdown, while Eddie Faulkner and former walk-on transfer Matt Unertl also added scoring runs. Wisconsin cruised to a 49-10 victory after outgaining the Racers 404-190 and holding better than an 11-minute edge in time of possession. Kavanagh was solid in his starting debut, completing 8-of-12 passes for 102 yards, while Bollinger saw his initial collegiate action and connected on 3-of-7 passes for 37 yards, including a six-yard scoring strike to Marcus Carpenter in the third quarter.

Dayne's one half of work allowed him to move into 14th place on the NCAA career rushing list with 4,698 yards (not counting bowl games). The countdown to the record had officially begun and already Alvarez was being questioned about how he decided to pull Dayne at halftime. His response: "It's just gut feeling. Just common sense. There was no reason to put Ron back in there in the second half. I felt that would have been humiliating to Ron and to Murray State at that point. There are 10 games left. There is a lot of football left. There will be games he will be carrying in the fourth quarter. Don't panic. Ron will get plenty of touches."

The fact was that everyone was doing the math. Each time the Badger coaches took Dayne out of a game early represented a missed opportunity to chip away at Williams' record. But Alvarez and his staff had always been averse to running up the score of a game or leaving a player like Dayne in just so he could pad statistics.

"Barry did a great job of framing it as a program Heisman and a program rushing record and that really was a motivator," said Brian White, who had taken over as UW's offensive coordinator in 1999. "You could do it with Ron because he was so unselfish and selfless, but it really was the platform that we used – you heard the quote a million times: 'the record will be broken in the context of the game.' We got criticized in writing that the only people who were going to prevent Ron Dayne from breaking the rushing record were the Wisconsin coaches because we didn't play him in the second half (against Murray State). And people were saying that those yards are going to be critical down the stretch once you get into the Big Ten and, those first four weeks, you need to pack the rushing yards because it's going to get harder once you get into the (conference) season.

"Our discussion was that we really believed with the defense that we had and the team that we had in '99 that we could win the Big Ten championship and that was the most critical component. As long as we were winning, Ron was going to be one of the critical reasons why we were winning. We were very unsettled at quarterback until Brooks took over in that Ohio State game, so we knew that the offensive line and Ron were going to have to really carry the offensive part of the team and the defense was going to have to really play well and we were great in special teams again, particularly with Nick Davis and the return game.

"The mindset was that the Heisman and all the accolades would take care of themselves provided that Ron stayed healthy and that we kept winning, and we did not compromise that. We were criticized throughout the process by national media, local media, everybody, but Ron understood. We told him there were not going to be garbage yards. We'd be sick to our stomach if it's 38-0 or 45-7 in some of those games that we played and Ron gets hurt in the third or fourth quarter of a game when the game was out of reach."

Andy Baggot of the *Wisconsin State Journal* was among those who were skeptical of the Badger coaches' use of Dayne.

"I was critical of Barry," Baggot said. "He had a chance to own one of the greatest records of all time – why are you pulling the reins back on him? But in retrospect, he did it the right way. And I think that's why it bothered me so much that at the end of that season there were people saying Ron Dayne is winning [the Heisman] only as a lifetime achievement award when, in fact, his team won. He set the record honorably, he didn't get any garbage time, he didn't do anything like that. He did it in a tough conference against tough competition down the stretch. He did it by having to overcome some adversity. In the Cincinnati game he fumbled, they lost, everyone was on his back. They lost to Michigan the following week. He got his feet back under him and won it. I wrote a column at that time basically saying this guy deserves the Heisman for many things, but one of them is it was done in the context of teamwork, it was done within the context of a championship-winning performance and it was done in the context of good sportsmanship, because they did it contrary to what I had called for at the time, which was letting him carry the ball rather than taking him out when the game was in hand."

Dayne was fine with things as long as the Badgers were winning.

"I'd get in and maybe have two touchdowns and a hundred-some yards and be done," Dayne said. "We could have run up the score and I could have run for a lot more yards. But I was trying to get out, I guess, so I could sit back and watch the other guys play. Especially if we had the lead, it didn't bother me at all."

Dayne and the Badgers, who had moved up to eighth in the *USA Today*/ESPN coaches poll (they remained ninth in the Associated Press poll) after the win over Murray State, returned to Camp Randall Stadium the following Saturday to host a Ball State team that had lost its opener at Indiana the previous week. Dayne, who had been overtaken by Warrick in the Scripps Howard Heisman voters poll after the Murray State game, entered the Ball State game needing 364 yards to break Archie Griffin's Big Ten rushing record (the Big Ten included bowl game statistics). He got his yards, but they did not come as easily as most thought they would.

Wisconsin used a Vitaly Pisetsky field goal, a safety and a 77-yard kickoff return for a touchdown by Davis to move out to a 12-0 lead after the first quarter. Linebacker Chris Ghidorzi scored on a 25-yard interception return in the second quarter, and Pisetsky added a 53-yard field goal just before halftime for a 22-7 Badger lead at the intermission. The offense, however, had not scored a touchdown, and Dayne had been "limited" to 98 yards on 20 carries, while Kavanagh completed only 3-of-7 passes for 29 yards. Wisconsin blew the game open in the second half by scoring 21 unanswered points and going on to a 50-10 victory. Dayne finished with 158 yards and a touchdown on 31 attempts. The performance raised his career total (bowls not included) to 4,856 yards, good for

11th place on the all-time NCAA list. In his quest for the conference rushing record, which included bowl games, Dayne moved into second place behind Griffin with 5,384 yards.

"He's so big and strong," Ball State coach Bill Lynch said after the game. "What they do, with his style, is perfect. The thing that I noticed on the sideline is how patient he is. He doesn't jump out on his own. He stays in there and he trusts his offensive line and then when that seam pops, he finds it. That's about as good as you're going to play because he's so patient. Some backs want to jump out there and do it all on their own, but he has great patience and great trust in his offensive line, which he should because they are really good."

Dayne's offensive line, of course, included veterans McIntosh, Ferrario, Costa and Rabach, now all long-time starters. Gibson's replacement at right tackle, however, was first-year starter Mark Tauscher, who had been McIntosh's backup on the left side for three years. Tauscher graduated in the spring of 1999, made a trip to the Kentucky Derby and was contemplating attending Youngstown State, where he could play one more year of college football. The Badger coaches did not realize Tauscher had one more year of eligibility remaining. They tracked him down and convinced him to return to Madison to play one final season. It would prove to be a life-changing move for Tauscher, who went on to a lengthy and successful career with the Green Bay Packers.

On the same day that Dayne was churning out his 158 yards against Ball State, other early-season Heisman contenders were making their marks, as well. Georgia Tech quarterback Joe Hamilton completed 22 of 25 passes for 387 yards, four touchdowns and no interceptions as the Yellow Jackets lost 41-35 at No. 1-ranked Florida State. And Brees connected on 24 of 40 through the air for 317 yards and a touchdown in Purdue's 28-23 win over Notre Dame.

Next up for the Badgers was an unranked Cincinnati team that most figured would simply serve as a final tune-up before the huge Big Ten opener the following week at home against Michigan. It was anything but a tune-up. Dayne sustained an ankle sprain in the first quarter and spent the rest of the game being spelled by Faulkner. Despite the injury, Dayne played courageously and ended up with his highest rushing total – 231 yards and a touchdown on 28 carries – of the season. The Bearcats, however, held a stunning 7-6 edge at the half and went ahead, 14-6, midway through the third quarter. Dayne's 18-yard scoring run later in the third period brought the Badgers to within 14-12, but Kavanagh's pass for a two-point conversion was negated by a holding penalty. Wisconsin did not score again, though the Badgers had chances. Cincinnati fumbled a Kevin Stemke punt halfway through the fourth quarter, leaving Wisconsin first and 10 at the Bearcat 15-yard line with 8:12 left to play. Dayne picked up five yards to set up second down and five. Dayne got the call again and dragged Cincinnati defenders toward the end zone for what looked to be another of his amazing touchdown runs. But Bearcat Bobby Fuller knocked the ball loose as Dayne was stretching for the goal line and Cincinnati recovered in its own end zone. The Bearcats added a field goal for a 17-12 lead, but Wisconsin still had another shot. The Badgers took over at their own 20-yard line with 5:01 remaining and drove to the Cincinnati 14 with 16 seconds left. Kavanagh proceeded to hit Lee Evans with a touchdown pass, but it was brought back due to an illegal motion call on Badger tight end John Sigmund. The Badgers' uncharacteristically high eighth and final penalty sealed their fate. They had dominated Cincinnati statistically, but had come up short where it counted the most.

What should have been one of the proudest days of Dayne's career – he eclipsed Griffin's career conference rushing mark in the loss at Cincinnati – was, to say the least, bittersweet. The Badgers plummeted nine spots to 17th in the Associated Press poll the following Monday with fourth-ranked Michigan coming to town. And

Dayne began to sink on the numerous Heisman Trophy "watch lists" being kept by media outlets around the country. Bruce Hooley of the *Cleveland Plain Dealer* ranked Dayne fourth behind Warrick, Brees and Hamilton and wrote, "Sore ankle and key fumble in loss to Cincinnati hurt his chances." He fell to third in the Scripps Howard poll, just ahead of Brees. The conference opener at home against the Wolverines, with ESPN's College Gameday show in Madison to make the game a national focal point, would be a prime opportunity for Dayne to again silence the skeptics. Dayne admitted as much.

"I'll never remember the Big Ten record as much as [that] I fumbled and we lost the game," he told reporters as the Michigan game loomed. "I know I need a great game against Michigan to make up for it."

What Dayne had against the Wolverines, however, was a solid half but nothing more. He ran for 88 yards on 14 carries before the break, including a fine 34-yard touchdown run that cut the Wolverines' lead to 14-9 at halftime. Michigan's Tom Brady threw an 8-yard touchdown pass to Aaron Shea to open the scoring before Wolverine wide receiver David Terrell scored on a 45-yard double reverse for a 14-0 lead after one quarter. But the Badgers bounced back with a Pisetsky field goal and Dayne's run. It was the second half, however, where Dayne's Heisman hopes and the Badgers' dreams of a Big Ten title repeat appeared to near the edge of the cliff. Dayne had eight carries for zero yards after halftime as Michigan limited Wisconsin to just 54 net yards from the start of the second half until the Badgers' final possession – an 80-yard scoring drive engineered by Bollinger, who had replaced an injured Kavanagh early in the fourth quarter. The bright spot in the 21-16 loss, however, was Bollinger, whose competitiveness and athletic ability had given Wisconsin a chance late in the game. He had guided the Badgers down the field and capped the drive with a 13-yard touchdown run.

"I didn't think I was going to play, but Kav got hurt and we were down and I came in, got a little spark and we almost came back," Bollinger recalled. "I think we got stopped on a fourth and one (early in the fourth quarter). We couldn't quite complete the comeback. But it was fun for me to be in Camp Randall, 2:30, ABC game. It was the first time I had been on the field for a game that was the real deal. I remember moments: we had moved the ball right down the field, kind of hurry-up mode, made a couple plays and they called a quarterback draw, we must have been on the 10-yard line (actually the 13). We break the huddle and Ron says, 'Just follow me.' And I'm thinking 'I don't know where I'm going, buddy, I'm just running.' But we ended up scoring on that play."

Wisconsin lost what was, at the time, a critical game. It was a pivotal point in the season with a number of sub-plots playing themselves out.

Crucial to the remainder of the season, it turns out, was Bollinger's emergence against Michigan. Lightly recruited out of Grand Forks, Bollinger was the prototypical "gym rat," a coach's son – his father, Rob, was an assistant football coach at the University of North Dakota – who was a terrific all-around athlete and who played all the key leadership positions (football quarterback, basketball point guard, baseball shortstop) on the high school sports teams of which he was a part. His performance in the fourth quarter against the Wolverines convinced Alvarez he had to give the redshirt freshman a shot. The tough part would be telling Kavanagh he had lost his starting job, but Kavanagh handled it like a coach would hope a senior would.

"It wasn't difficult," Kavanagh said. "Brooks was without a doubt the best quarterback for that team. I'll go to my grave with that. He was a really good guy. The football team was a heckuva lot bigger than I was. Was it something you want to go through your senior year and that type of thing? No. But, at the same time, I loved playing on that football team and I feel fortunate to have had the opportunity to play here. That was my role. And I wanted to do everything I possibly could to help him out and help the team out and I think I did that. It was a really valuable experience to go through and I think I grew up a lot because of it and it was part of the reason I decided to pursue the coaching thing for a while (Kavanagh was a college football coach for several years after his playing days at Wisconsin were over). Sometimes people think team chemistry means that everybody was best friends and I don't think that has anything to do with it. Did we all like each other? Yeah, we did. But, to me, team chemistry is knowing your role and accepting it. And that's what [the 1998 and 1999 Badgers] had."

As for Dayne, his lack of second-half production against Michigan was costing him dearly in the court of public opinion. Michael Vega of the *Boston Globe* wrote that Dayne "seemed to fall out of contention for the Heisman over the weekend" and that "if the Dayne Train expects to arrive at the Downtown Athletic Club in New York in December, he'll have to take the subway." The Scripps Howard poll, the one that actually consisted of Heisman Trophy voters and which Dayne led when the season started, dropped him from its top five, which now consisted of Warrick, Brees, Hamilton, Alabama running back Shaun Alexander and Arrington. The questions about Dayne's ability to produce in big games against quality opponents persisted.

If a two-game losing streak, questions at quarterback and external doubts about their All-American tailback weren't enough for the Badgers to contend with, then certainly the health of their head coach was. Alvarez had been having trouble with his right knee since March. He had arthritis and had the knee scoped a few times, but had been told by his doctor that he was likely facing a knee replacement at some point. The knee got worse during fall camp in 1999 and Alvarez began using crutches and a golf cart to maneuver around at practice. Prior to the start of the season opener against Murray State, Alvarez felt more pain in the knee and watched as it swelled, filling up with blood. Team physician Ben Graf drained the knee in the McClain Center training room. Alvarez spent the second half of the Murray State game watching from the Camp Randall Stadium press box. He was on crutches at Cincinnati as well, and missed his normal Monday news conference following the loss to the Bearcats because he was in Rochester, Minnesota, having the knee examined by doctors at the Mayo Clinic. The conclusion, again, was that he needed a knee replacement, so surgery was scheduled for Tuesday, October 5. When the doctors opened up Alvarez's knee that day, however, they saw that it was infected and delayed the replacement surgery until after the season. Alvarez would miss the Badgers' October 9 game at Minnesota, watching instead from his room at the Mayo Clinic.

So, with their head coach ailing and both their running back's Heisman Trophy chances and their opportunity to repeat as conference champions in jeopardy, the Badgers traveled to one of the toughest venues in college football – Ohio Stadium – to face Coach John Cooper's 12th-ranked Ohio State Buckeyes. Alvarez's first win at Wisconsin over a ranked opponent had come, ironically, against 12th-ranked Ohio State in 1992. But that game was played in Camp Randall Stadium. The degree of difficulty figured to be much greater in Columbus where the Badgers had won just four times since 1914. Dayne entered the game needing 1,105 yards to break Williams' record and was just two yards behind Ohio State's Griffin on the career NCAA rushing list. He needed to average 157.9 yards per game over the final seven contests to reach the record.

Considering what ultimately transpired, the first 25 minutes of the game were something of a disaster for the Badgers. Michael Wiley scored on a 1-yard run. Dan Stultz booted a 35-yard field goal. And when Reggie Germany caught a 40-yard touchdown pass from quarterback Steve Bellisari with 10:23 remaining in the first half, Ohio State already had a 17-0 lead. Trailing by 17 points is the last situation a team wants to find itself in, particularly on the road at a place like Ohio State. It was doubly tough for the Badgers because their grinding, physical running game wasn't conducive to a quick-strike comeback.

But Bollinger, a surprise starter to everyone outside the Wisconsin program, gave the Badgers the second offensive option – aside from Dayne – that they had been looking for. Throwing the ball, running the option, giving to Dayne and helping to keep the Buckeyes' defense more honest than it would have been had Dayne been the only threat, Bollinger had Wisconsin moving the ball late in the second quarter. A pair of scoring drives resulted in two Vitaly Pisetsky field goals that cut the Ohio State lead to 17-6 at the half. Years later Dayne recalled the scene in the Badger locker room. "Coach was throwing [his crutches] and going off," Dayne said. "It was quiet the whole time in the locker room, there wasn't anybody saying anything. On the way out, it was like 'Come on guys, we gotta do it, let's do it.'" And that's what they did.

Wiley took Pisetsky's kickoff to begin the second half, started upfield and had the ball knocked loose by Wisconsin's Ryan Marks. Bobby Myers recovered it at the Ohio State 14-yard line for the Badgers, and Wisconsin's season was never the same. Dayne scored from three yards out two plays later and went in on an 11-yard run up the middle (after a Bollinger audible) on the Badgers' next possession. Wisconsin led 18-17 and never trailed again. Pisetsky added a field goal, Dayne scored two more touch-downs and Faulkner contributed a scoring run as the Badgers tallied 42 unanswered points for a stunning 42-17 victory. It was clearly a turning-point victory and the emotional postgame lock-er room scene reflected the game's significance.

"It was probably one of the biggest turnarounds I've ever seen," Alvarez said. "To be down 17-0, get on the board late in the first half, to dominate them like that, 42 unanswered points in the second half, in Columbus, and a good team – that was a nice team. That was unbelievable. I'll never forget (UW Director of Athletics) Pat Richter after the game. He came down – it's the only time he ever asked to talk to the team. He was so proud of the team and he broke down crying talking to the team afterwards."

White recalled telling some of the Badgers during their week of practice that Ohio State was a good team, but that legends like Griffin and Hopalong Cassidy would not be on the field.

"One of the things we coined that week was 'we're not playing the ghosts of Ohio State past,'" White said. "We're not playing Archie Griffin and we're not playing Hopalong Cassidy; you're not playing all these great players at Ohio State. We're playing Ohio State in 'the Horseshoe.' Play the players that are on the field, watch the film and trust the fact that we're better and can beat Ohio State in that stadium. So that was the mantra all week and our players believed it. And we go out and it's 17-0 before you could shake a stick. I remember sitting up in the press box saying 'Oh my God, those ghosts have appeared.' And right before the half, Brooks went on a great two-minute drive and we kicked the field goal and it's 17-6 at that time. We knocked the ball loose on the opening kickoff, Ron scored to make it 17-12 and then the floodgates just opened. They self-destructed and we ran the heck out of the ball and Brooks played great. It was as fulfilling a game as I've ever been a part of. The emotion in the locker room after the game was incredible because Barry had told the players before the game what was going to happen (regarding his knee surgery). Pat Richter was in the locker room and Pat had tears in his eyes. It was pretty special."

Dayne ended up with 161 yards and four touchdowns on 32 carries. He had surpassed both Griffin and Georgia's Herschel Walker on the NCAA career rushing list. Bollinger completed 15 passes for 167 yards and ran for another 78 yards, opening up the field for the entire offense. "That was a good old-fashioned butt kicking," Cooper said after the game. "You have to give Wisconsin credit. They kept the ball away from us in the second half. We could not stop them in the second half. When we fumbled the second-half kickoff, we gave them the momentum."

Dayne said after the Ohio State game that he wasn't trying to prove anything to anyone but, try or not, he did. Again. He proved doubters wrong with his performance against UCLA in the Rose Bowl nine months earlier and he proved them wrong with his showing against Ohio State. And, as ABC play-by-play man Brad Nessler said after Dayne's 46-yard run in the fourth quarter against the Buckeyes, "Ron Dayne has just rumbled his way back into the Heisman race."

That Heisman race was being led by Warrick who, on the same day that Dayne re-emerged at Ohio State, caught three touchdown passes and threw one himself in a win over Duke. But Warrick's candidacy ended abruptly the following week when he was suspended for two games after being arrested. That left Dayne and players like Brees, Hamilton, Alexander and Marshall's Chad Pennington to battle it out for the rest of the season.

Wisconsin, back in the Associated Press' top 25 at No. 20, faced a road game at 25th-ranked Minnesota. The team would battle the Gophers without Alvarez, who remained hospitalized at the Mayo Clinic. Dayne gained just 80 yards and scored once against the Golden Gophers, but the Badgers gutted out a 20-17 overtime victory that ended when Pisetsky booted a 31-yard field goal. Bollinger picked up 62 yards on the ground and threw for 212, continuing to hurt opponents like the Gophers who loaded up to stop Dayne.

Alvarez returned to the program in time for the Badgers' Homecoming matchup with Indiana on October 16. Dayne needed 864 yards to catch Williams and he had five games left in which to do it. He had something else, as well. *Sports Illustrated*'s B.J. Schecter compiled a list of the "Top 10 Disappointments" of the 1999 college football season and listed Dayne at No. 6. Schecter wrote, "The 5'10", 252-pound senior has rushed for 853 yards, but the Great Dayne hasn't been so great in the clutch. He fumbled two yards shy of the end zone in the fourth quarter of a 17-12 defeat at Cincinnati and was held to zero yards in the second half of the Badgers' 21-16 loss to Michigan." Dayne cut out the list and taped it to the inside of his locker where it served as an occasional motivator.

"Sometimes coming from practice or going to practice, I'd be like 'I don't want to practice today,'" Dayne said. "And I'd look over at [that list]."

On the morning of the Badgers' game with Indiana, Andy Baggot of the *Wisconsin State Journal* wrote that "things are looking pretty iffy right now where Ron Dayne and his pursuit of the NCAA record book is concerned." Baggot noted that Dayne would need to average 172.8 yards per game over his final five games – a very tall order – to break the national rushing mark. Baggot went on to explain that, due to a number of factors weighing in Dayne's favor, he believed the running back could do it. But, Baggot wrote, "the final push has to start right here, right now."

Wisconsin and Dayne made quick work of the Hoosiers, cruising to a 38-0 halftime lead and going on to win 59-0. Dayne rushed for 167 yards and a pair of touchdowns on only 17 carries (a 9.8 yards-per-carry average) before leaving the game after the first half. The performance allowed him to become just the fourth player in NCAA Division I history (joining North Carolina's Amos Lawrence, Pittsburgh's Tony Dorsett and New Mexico State's Denvis Manns) to rush for at least 1,000 yards in four different seasons. The Badgers set a school record with a remarkable 705 yards in total offense against the Hoosiers. Asked after the game about pulling Dayne so early, Alvarez noted that Dayne had injured a finger at Minnesota the week prior, but he also stuck to his long-time philosophy of not elevating an individual above the rest of the team.

"We were going to give him a couple of carries before the end of the half, but Ron's got a bad finger and I thought it would be foolish for us, just for yardage sake, to put him in the game," Alvarez told reporters. "I just didn't feel that was the proper thing to do."

Local media seemed to disagree. Baggot wrote after the blowout of Indiana, "Somewhere down the line, Dayne and this duel with history have to become more of a priority. The pursuit of a Big Ten title is job one, of course, but Dayne should be a close second on the to-do list for the Badgers. If some feelings are temporarily hurt on the other sidelines, so be it. If it means temporarily elevating the agenda of an individual over that of the team, fine."

But Alvarez did not panic, and he did not put Dayne on a pedestal above his teammates. And Dayne was just fine with that.

"Ron just went out and played," Alvarez said. "Outwardly he never worried about records, he never worried about how many yards he had, how many times he was going to carry the ball. At times, I called him the reluctant hero. We'd put something in where, because of the formation and how people would adjust, we knew we could give him the ball and get him to the safety. It was going to be a big play and if the safety didn't tackle him it was going to be a home run. A lot of times I'd be up in the (press) box and I'd say 'do it now' and I'd look on the field and Eddie Faulkner would be on the field – Ronnie would take himself out. You think about his senior year, everybody was complaining I was pulling him out of the games and I was taking him out of the games early and I wanted him to break the record in the context of the game and not just padding up runs, and I didn't want to get him hurt. He never complained one time."

Dayne was back in the Heisman Trophy race to be sure, but he was still running a distant fourth in the Scripps Howard poll. Hamilton, Alexander and Brees were all well ahead of Dayne as the now 17th-ranked Badgers prepared for what, on paper, looked to be one of their stiffest tests of the season: an 11th-ranked Michigan State team that was leading the nation in run defense, allowing a paltry 39.9 yards per game.

Each week during the season, sports information director Steve Malchow produced a news release for the media. The packet contained notes about the Badgers along with a variety of statistical information. Disappointed in reading lists like the one that appeared in *Sports Illustrated* and in listening to analysts say things about Dayne he felt were untrue, Malchow debuted a new page in the release he distributed on October 18, two days after the Indiana game.

"I was sitting home one evening watching a sports TV show, or a couple of them, and the reporters were saying things about Ron that weren't accurate," Malchow said. "I was fuming when I heard the things they were saying. 'Well, those two games came against lousy competition' and 'He's just a big back with no speed' and 'He's a three-yards-and-a-cloud-of-dust guy.' The more I heard these things, I got to thinking that's not true at all. He has a number of long plays. So I wondered how I could change what people were believing about him and that's where I came up with the concept of myths and facts. It ended up catching fire in a couple major publications. The simplicity of it was kind of funny; I didn't think it was all that earth-shattering but it gave me a chance to debunk some of the myths out there. And that whole concept kind of tied in a little bit to what got me thinking about the Michigan State game being the key game, because there was a myth out there that Ron's good games only came against poor competition. And there was the myth that Barry was piling up big yardage by extra carries against the bad teams. And I looked at that Michigan State game as, 'Okay, you want formidable competition, here's the best defense in the country in terms of the rush.' If Ron can have a big game there, wow, that could debunk that myth in a hurry."

The new page in the release previewing the Michigan State game was called "What's Myth and What's Fact?" Malchow took aim at several of the myths about Dayne that the media was buying into:

Myth: Ron Dayne turns the ball over.

Facts: In 1,058 carries, Dayne has suffered just eight fumbles lost. That is one miscue for every 132.3 carries. Dayne has fumbled on just 0.7 percent of his *career* carries. Texas' Ricky Williams, for comparison, had 12 fumbles lost during his Heisman Trophy-winning *season*.

Myth: Ron Dayne hasn't gained yardage vs. quality opposition.

Facts: Dayne and the Badgers have faced nationally-ranked foes 13 times since 1996. His average rushing yards per game in those contests is 99.1. Included in that average was a 46-yard performance vs. Syracuse when he played with a stinger (only 13 carries), a 24-yard effort vs. Iowa when he sprained an ankle on the first series of the game (seven carries) and 36 yards vs. Georgia when the Badgers fell behind 19-0 by halftime (11 carries).

Dayne has recorded games of 136, 126 and 95 yards vs. Penn State when the Nittany Lions were rated third, sixth and 14th nationally. He also had 139 yards vs. #14 Northwestern (1996), 246 vs. #6 UCLA (1999) and 161 vs. #12 Ohio State (1999). Additionally, Dayne's career average per game in Big Ten contests (142.1) is fairly close to his norm in non-conference action (151.5).

Myth: Ron Dayne has had a disappointing 1999 season.

Facts: Dayne has rushed for 1,020 yards with four games left.

He ranks sixth nationally in rushing despite facing defenses every week geared to slow him. Dayne reached 1,000 yards faster in 1999 than any of his previous seasons despite sitting out six quarters in blowout victories. His average of 145.7 yards per game is higher than his career norm entering '99.

Malchow's simple and direct effort drew praise from national media. Tom Luicci of the *Newark Star-Ledger* called it "one of the best Heisman campaigns ever," noting that unlike some of the gimmicky efforts of the past, "this one required a little more thought."

But all of the news releases and promotional push in the world wouldn't help Dayne if he did not keep producing on the field. The 11:10 a.m. kickoff at Camp Randall Stadium ensured that if Dayne had a big day in the nationally televised (ESPN2) contest against the Spartans, the highlights would be shown again and again throughout the afternoon and well into the evening. That turned out to be the case.

Michigan State was forced to punt on its first series, leaving the Badgers to take over at their own 13-yard line with 11:09 left in the first quarter. Four plays, 87 yards and 1:28 later, Wisconsin led 7-0. Bollinger completed a 15-yard pass to tight end Mark Anelli on the first play before Dayne picked up a total of 21 yards rushing on the next two. Dayne then took a handoff from Bollinger at the Wisconsin 49, bolted through a huge hole produced by Ferrario, McIntosh, Rabach and tight end Dague Retzlaff, and outran three Michigan State defenders to the end zone for the 65th touchdown of his career. Dayne had carried three times on the first drive and gained 72 yards, 32 more than the Spartans had been allowing per game. Wisconsin led 23-3 at halftime, with Dayne having chewed up the Spartan defense for 152 yards and a pair of scores. He finished with 34 carries for 214 yards and two touchdowns as the Badgers pummeled the Spartans 40-10. Wisconsin ran for 301 yards to go with just 59 yards through the air. Alvarez's 66th coaching victory at Wisconsin (which made him the winningest coach in school history) was a "statement game," for both Dayne and the team in general.

"We felt like we could run the ball," Alvarez said of the 1999 Michigan State win. "We thought our guys were tougher than their guys. I can remember (ESPN2 analyst) Bill Curry asking me on Friday whether I thought we could run the ball against them. I said, 'Oh no, no one can run the ball (on the Spartans). But we'll probe a little bit.' Our guys jumped on them quickly and really went after them and they didn't respond to us, they didn't come back at us. That was really a show. Our guys put on a show." (Curry, who played collegiately and professionally and coached at the college level, sensed what Alvarez meant by "probe" when he predicted prior to the game that Alvarez would eventually try to take Dayne and "go right at [the Spartans] and try to grind them into submission." Clearly, Curry was right.)

Brian White knew Alvarez enjoyed the moment.

"We just kept running the ball and Barry was great," White said. "He was up in the press box for all those games and he said just keep probing them with the run. That was his little slogan. He was having fun up there – it was pretty neat."

Dayne's performance moved him ahead of USC's Charles White and into third place on the all-time rushing list with 5,797 yards. It gave him his eleventh 200-yard game, a Big Ten-record. And it moved him up to second in the Scripps Howard Heisman voters' poll. Dayne was once again a prime contender and needed to average 161 yards in his last three games to break Williams' record.

Michigan State coach Nick Saban summed up Dayne nicely during his postgame news conference when he was asked if Dayne was the best running back he had coached against.

"In his own way, probably yes," responded Saban. "There have been some other guys who have been a little more flashy sometimes because of their great speed or big play ability. But down in and down out, Dayne's a tough guy to deal with all day long and a tough guy to tackle. He's about as good as anybody I've ever seen. You have to play to stop him almost all the time."

The 11th-ranked Badgers followed the huge win over Michigan State with a 35-19 victory at Northwestern on October 30. Dayne added 162 yards and a pair of touchdowns to his total, leaving him 321 yards from the record with two games left to play. The first of the final two contests, at Purdue on November 6, would help to define a running back. The second game helped to define an athletic program.

"I thought [the Michigan State game] was probably the key turnaround game of the whole year for making him a viable candidate," Malchow said of Dayne. "The other game might have been two weeks after that at Purdue. What I remember about that was although I didn't agree that Drew Brees was the top competition for the award, I knew that the television networks and the *Sports Illustrated*s and the *USA Today*s would create that situation where that game was Heisman candidate vs. Heisman candidate. My feeling was that was another showcase opportunity of Dayne vs. Brees. And if Ron could have a big game in that game, he could effectively knock Brees out of the competition and he could climb one more spot. We had talked earlier that my personal goal for Ron was to have a great season as a team, knowing he would get a lot of credit for that, and hopefully he could get to New York. When he fell off the map after the Cincinnati game, I thought Michigan State and Purdue, no question, were the two opportunities to get back on the list and even climb the list."

Malchow was correct. The game was billed as a matchup of Dayne vs. Brees, the two Heisman candidates. Herb Gould of the *Chicago Sun-Times* wrote that the game "has the potential to be a college football classic." He had good reason for those sentiments. The game would be a rematch of the wildly entertaining 1998 contest between the two schools, during which Brees completed 55 of

83 passes, but was on the losing end at Camp Randall Stadium, thanks in part to Jamar Fletcher's second-half interception return for a touchdown. This time around, the 10th-ranked Badgers, 5-1 in conference play, were fighting to remain in the hunt for the Big Ten title. (Penn State was 5-0 and playing host to Minnesota.) The No. 17 Boilermakers were still in contention for a top-tier bowl game.

The spotlight on Dayne and Brees revealed two individuals with different personal backgrounds who played in different offensive styles. But Dayne and Brees, who had met a few months earlier in August at the Big Ten Media Day in Chicago, became friends and remain so. Both players were humble and always put team success ahead of their own accomplishments.

A beautiful, 63-degree fall day greeted the Badgers and Boilermakers at Ross-Ade Stadium and so did the stunning news that Minnesota had knocked off previously unbeaten and No. 2-ranked Penn State, 24-23, on a last-second field goal earlier in the afternoon. A Wisconsin victory in West Lafayette would put the Badgers in a tie for first place with the Nittany Lions with one week remaining in the season.

Wisconsin and Purdue played a scoreless first quarter before the two teams traded second-quarter touchdowns. Ironically, the Badgers' opening tally came on a pass from Bollinger to Retzlaff from three yards out, while Purdue's score came via a one-yard run from Brees. But Wisconsin always had an answer for the Boilermakers on this day and the first one came courtesy of Nick Davis. Davis had already returned three punts and one kickoff for touchdowns in less than two years as a Badger, but he was about to add another. The Boilermakers kicked off to Davis who caught the ball at the Wisconsin 9-yard line. He got a huge hole to run through, helped by a nice block from Michael Bennett, then beat Boilermaker kicker Travis Dorsch and outraced every-one to the end zone for a 91-yard return that provided Wisconsin with a 14–7 halftime lead. Despite the score, Purdue held a sizeable statistical advantage, including outrushing the Badgers 84–79 during the first two quarters. The Boilermakers, who had run 21 more plays than the Badgers, had held Dayne to 77 yards on 13 carries.

In retrospect, Dayne may have won the Heisman Trophy with his second-half performance that day against Purdue. The Boilermakers came back to tie it at 14–14 when Brees threw an 11-yard touchdown pass to Tim Stratton with 5:21 left in the third quarter. Wisconsin punted on its next possession and Purdue used nine plays to march to the Wisconsin 19-yard line with a chance to take the lead. The Boilermakers opted for a reverse pass that had receiver Vinny Sutherland throwing into the end zone where Badger defensive back Bobby Myers made a critical interception. The Badgers took over at their own 20 and Bollinger went to work, passing Wisconsin out to its own 47 where Dayne made his presence felt. He carried for a total of 12 yards on the next two plays before taking a handoff from Bollinger on first down from the Purdue 41. Dayne followed fullback Chad Kuhns around the right side, got a block from Retzlaff, turned upfield and won a foot-race to the end zone for a touchdown that put the Badgers ahead, 21–14, with 11:14 remaining. The run gave Dayne 186 yards in a game in which he had already passed Dorsett for second place on the NCAA career rushing list. There was, however, more to come.

Reminiscent of the Wisconsin-Purdue game from a year earlier, Fletcher picked off a Brees pass and ran it back 34 yards for a touchdown to give the Badgers a two-touchdown lead with just 4:43 left to play. But Brees was not finished. He quickly guided his team back down the field on its next possession, capping the 13-play, 64-yard drive with his second one-yard scoring run of the game. It was not over yet. The Badgers recovered Dorsch's onside kick at the Purdue 46. The Boilermakers had used all of their time-outs, but Wisconsin would still need to make a first down to lock up the game. Dayne picked up a yard on the first play before defining himself, the championship Badgers of 1998 and 1999, and Wisconsin football during the Alvarez era on the next run. He took a handoff from Bollinger on second-and nine and carried the ball outside to the left with Kuhns ahead of him. Purdue linebacker Mike Rose got a hand on Dayne, who stumbled but stayed on his feet, before Ferrario eliminated him from the play. Kuhns glanced off free safety Adrian Beasley and fell to the ground, leaving Beasley and Dayne to meet head-on. It was no contest. Dayne bulled over Beasley, essentially throwing him out of the way with his right arm. Dayne continued up-field where he met linebacker Jason Loerzel at the Purdue 42-yard line. He dragged Loerzel to the 36 for a first down. Brad Nessler and Bob Griese, who handled the play-by-play for ABC that day, were duly impressed.

"Now that's a big-time run," Nessler told the viewing audience. "It's only 10 yards and maybe won't make all the highlight clips, but that's one tough son of a gun." Griese added, "You've got no chance if you try to tackle him above the waist." It was vintage Dayne and it typified the style of football Alvarez had learned growing up in western Pennsylvania and eventually brought to Wisconsin.

"That's how we played," Alvarez said. "That's how I learned the game. When I went to Nebraska, that's the style we played. It was a very physical, ball possession, field position type game. And I know how to play that type of game. After studying and watching people around me as I left Nebraska as a high school coach, the teams that would come in and beat them always were more physical than they were. It's hard to imagine anyone more physical than Nebraska, but the ones that beat them, that's how they did it. They didn't come in there and be cute, they had to be more physical. So when I took this job – you know if I took a different job in a different part of the country where you could get more skilled athletes than linemen, then you've got to go to a different type of game. But here, it was linemen first, tough guys on defense, linebackers. I knew I could get them and try to find the best skill players for the most part outside the state."

Dayne happened to be a rare combination of everything Alvarez was looking for. He was big, tough and skilled and his exclamation-point of a run on the final drive in West Lafayette had finally put him over the hump or, as the headline on the *Wisconsin State Journal*'s sports section read the next day: "On destiny's doorstep."

"That was a defining moment," Alvarez said of Dayne's performance at Purdue. "That was a Heisman game – him and Drew Brees – that was a great game. Brees played well. They scored and Nick Davis ran a kick back. Every time they'd do something, our guys responded. But now we've got the ball late in the game, and this is what I liked about our good teams. We could burn six or seven minutes if we had to – we could hold onto that ball. You don't get a chance to win the game. You don't want Brees and Purdue to have the ball in their hands late in the game with a chance to win, so we're trying to run the clock out. And that one run of his – they've got a safety come up on him and he hits him like he's a little boy, just throws him out of the way and keeps on running. I think that opened everyone's eyes. It was crunch time against a good team, everything's on the line and this guy took over the game."

White felt it was not only a defining moment, but the moment Dayne locked up something more.

"He was reckless," White said of Dayne's final carry against the Boilermakers. "That was the Heisman showdown game. Ron had cycled himself back into the Heisman discussion through his performance at Ohio State and that was kind of the exclamation point – he won the Heisman Trophy with that performance. He was unbelievable in the game and that run was just – I know his record-breaking run will always be his signature run – but if there's a second run in his career that will forever be burned in my brain it'll be that run against Purdue because it was such a significant first-down, just what he had to do to get it. It was just amazing."

Bollinger twice took a knee and the clock ran out. The Wisconsin and Purdue players and coaches met on the field to shake hands as Malchow escorted Dayne over to ABC sideline reporter Lynn Swann. Swann got two questions in to Dayne before Brees stepped in to greet the Badger running back and congratulate him. The Purdue star left Dayne by saying simply: "You deserve the Heisman."

The Badgers were now 8-2 overall, 6-1 in the Big Ten and locked in a tie for first place with Penn State, which still had games to play against Michigan and Michigan State. If the Badgers defeated Iowa at Camp Randall Stadium in their regular-season finale on November 13, they would be guaranteed a share of the conference title. If Wisconsin defeated the Hawkeyes and Penn State lost one of its last two games, then the Badgers would be outright conference champions and return to the Rose Bowl for a second consecutive season. Dayne's superlative per-formance at Purdue – 222 yards and a touchdown on 32 carries (nearly seven yards per attempt) – put him just 99 yards from breaking Ricky Williams' year-old career NCAA rushing mark.

CHAPTER EIGHT
Perfection

Brian White had coached, mentored and befriended Ron Dayne for the running back's entire four years at Wisconsin, but he almost missed his prized pupil's biggest day. White liked to go for a run on the mornings of Badger game days and, as Madison was waking up and preparing to witness history in Camp Randall Stadium on November 13, 1999, the Wisconsin offensive coordinator and running backs coach went out for his customary jog.

"I was crossing Dayton Street right over by the Kohl Center and it was a beautiful day," White said of his run the morning of the Wisconsin-Iowa game. "I always like to run on game day and get a little nervous energy out. It was a great week, an exciting week, and I was just kind of prancing around, not going too fast. I wasn't paying attention and I got blocked by one car coming across. I thought that I was free and I kept running and this car, by the grace of God, saw me at the last possible second, swerved away across the median and nothing happened. But my heart was pounding, just absolutely pounding from that, and I'm saying, 'Wow, there's someone looking out for me because that guy shouldn't have avoided me.'"

In retrospect, the way the remainder of the day went for White and the Badgers, he could have stood in the middle of freeway traffic and he would not have been hit. The 1999 game between Wisconsin and Iowa was equal parts Hollywood and heartland. It featured a fan base that had come to watch the coronation of a once-in-a-generation running back, as well as the ascent of an entire athletic department. It also had a surreal merging of events that produced a perfect afternoon still stamped on the hearts and minds of the 79,404 people in attendance and the thousands more who watched in family rooms, bars, hotels, alumni gatherings and restaurants across the country.

First, there were the scenarios.

"We had something like six different scenarios to plan for," said Vince Sweeney, external relations director at Wisconsin at the time. "He sets the record, he didn't set the record. We win, Penn State wins. We win, Penn State loses. We lose, Penn State wins. Going into the day, we had put together a variety of scenarios for the postgame ceremony. There were two main events: where would we end up in the standings regarding a Rose Bowl berth and would Ron Dayne set the NCAA rushing record? We knew we were going to roll a stage out there for the postgame and we had scripts for 4-6 postgame scenarios. You know … if Penn State won, Wisconsin won and Ron set the record, this is the program, and so on. I just remember that one of the scripts was the ultimate scenario."

UW athletic officials began to plan early in the week for how to handle whichever one of the scenarios played itself out.

"I remember a bunch of meetings the week of the game, right away from Monday on," said Kevin Kluender, then an assistant in the athletic marketing department. "It had become apparent it was going to happen, very likely. So, right away we were talking about the postgame. I remember being surprised at how detailed we were getting because I hadn't been here very long. It was the first time I had been exposed to all the intricacies, being careful about everything, understanding that everyone was going to be running onto the field and stuff like that. I also remember we had a lot of other things going on that day. I think it was Bucky Badger's 50th birthday, so that was already in play. I remember being excited about the fact that if the team won they would get the trophy on the field because the year prior they didn't. I was thinking that could be kind of a neat moment."

There was plenty to be excited about. In fact, Tom Mulhern of the *Wisconsin State Journal* suggested it may have been the biggest week in the history of Badger football. There was Dayne's push toward the record, as well as his run at the Heisman Trophy. It was Senior Day and Wisconsin was facing Iowa, its bitter rival. And the Badgers were going to have the chance to win back-to-back conference titles for the first time since 1896 and 1897.

Malchow recalls hoping Dayne would stay healthy enough the break Williams' record.

"One thing I remember thinking through the week was that we were on the doorstep here, PLEASE do not let him get hurt," Malchow said. "Finish the deal. Too much is invested. Too many people have worked too hard. These offensive linemen deserve to have him break the record, we've got to come together. Our fan base needs it."

Dayne stayed healthy that week and the first scenario everyone was hoping for – good weather – came in spades that Saturday morning. A 6:47 a.m. sunrise brought clear skies and temperatures just above freezing in Madison, but those figures rose steadily through the 40s, 50s and even into the mid-60s as game-time approached. A home football game at Wisconsin is an event unto itself. The stadium is nestled into a patch of land with residential neighborhoods across Breese Terrace to the west, the busy intersection of Monroe and Regent Streets to the south and the Camp Randall Memorial Sports Center (or Shell) to the east. The games themselves are just part of the celebration. Fans gather to tailgate and visit with friends in what is normally a festive atmosphere punctuated by plumes of smoke from grills, footballs being tossed about and the fired up UW Marching Band. This particular Saturday, however, was different.

"I usually get to the stadium about three hours before the game and most times you can drive right up," said longtime Wisconsin football radio play-by-play voice Matt Lepay. "There are some tailgaters out, some commotion, some traffic. That day, it took a while to get to the parking lot. There was such anticipation the whole week. It was a perfect day, almost 70 degrees, ridiculously nice outside. At the time, though, the buildup was as much about the record as it was about Wisconsin on the verge of, going into the game, at least clinching a tie. To me, of all the home games, that one had as much anticipation as I can remember. It was just electric. It took a while maneuvering through pedestrian traffic just to get my car into the lot. It was a scene I hadn't seen before or since. Close a couple times, but nothing quite like that."

Longtime Madison sportscaster Jay Wilson agreed.

"At that point I had covered Badger football for 25 years," Wilson said. "The routine is, you get to the game an hour and a half before it starts and you walk through tailgaters in the parking lot and around the stadium and it's always exciting, people are always having fun. But that day, from the moment you walked from your car to the stadium, you had the sense that it was something different. It was something special. People had an extra gleam in their eye. They had an extra spring in their step. And it was as much of a pride of the state of Wisconsin as anything because here was Wisconsin on the national stage."

The national stage brings with it a heavy demand for tickets, which had been reportedly going for as much as $200 earlier in the week and were now at $300 or more. Longtime fans remember the 1999 Wisconsin-Iowa game being one of the toughest tickets in Camp Randall Stadium history. But that didn't stop at least one fan from making a ticket-related goodwill gesture.

Neil Ament, a Wisconsin alumnus who was a photographer for the *Daily Cardinal* during his days as a student, was in Madison for the Badgers' game with Iowa. A friend had cancelled a previously scheduled trip to Madison, so Ament was left with a couple of end zone seats he figured he would sell. He could have easily pocketed a few hundred dollars in the seller's market outside the stadium. Instead, he made the day for a man and his son.

"A year prior, I was in St. Louis for a baseball game and Mark McGwire had homered in the first four games to start the season," Ament recalled. "The record was five games and the fifth game was a tough ticket. I was there with my step-son and we went over to Busch Stadium and started walking around. It was a similar scene to what Madison was before the 'Ron Dayne game' because whenever anybody appeared with tickets to sell, it was a mob scene and a bidding war. A guy walks up to us and asks us if we were looking to go to the game. I said yes and he says, 'These are Stan Musial's seats. He can't go to the game, so he asked me to find a parent and their child to give the tickets to. Enjoy the game.' They were pretty good seats. So, outside Camp Randall a year later it's a mob scene, but I remembered what had happened in St. Louis. I found a guy and his son and just recreated the whole thing. I just handed them the tickets and said, 'Enjoy the game.' I didn't tell them why, but hopefully they continued on what started with the Stan Musial tickets."

Whether selling tickets, giving them away or just heading to Madison with them already in hand, that November day was a special one for fans of Wisconsin football.

"We were at State Street Brats to watch the game," said longtime fan Butch Gebhardt. "Iowa was not very good, so we felt like we were going to win and he was going to set the record. The feeling inside State Street Brats was really special and you could sense it building. I love that walk from [State Street Brats] to the stadium. I stopped at a friend's tailgate. It was a beautiful day, we had some good food. There was a feeling of momentum among the fans."

Luke Behnke was just a freshman and still learning about the special environment created on a football Saturday in Madison.

"I was in the dorms at the time and was still getting used to how the games worked, what a great time game day is in Madison," Behnke said. "I remember we headed down to Breese Terrace because we had heard in the dorms that that was kind of the place to go. Maybe it was my friends and I were excited or just the general crowd, but there was so much electricity out there and people were so excited about what was going to happen that day. I didn't really understand at the time how exciting it was. It was the first year I was in school and it was the first football season for me. At the time I knew it was a great thing, but I didn't realize it was a once-in-a-lifetime thing to see. But we were excited about it and excited to see Ron hopefully break the record. Everybody had signs for Ron and they passed out those towels, of course. It was the talk of the entire day. There was definitely an electricity about the stadium."

As was the case for many of the Badgers' big games, ABC was in town to televise. The game was distributed to just 21 percent of the nation, with Washington at UCLA, Kansas State at Nebraska and Maryland at Florida State also airing regionally on ABC during the 2:30 p.m. CST window. The Wisconsin-Iowa game ended up with a final rating of 5.9, meaning that was the percentage of America's approximately 99,400,000 television households that watched the game. ABC's personnel could feel the electricity in Madison, as well.

"The night before, you could tell the town was on fire, that there was this sense that we're about to see something special," said Jon Corl, ABC's lead graphics coordinator that day. "We go to a lot of games year-in and year-out and you never saw that kind of energy."

Wisconsin's players, who had turned around what had once been thought by many outside the program to be a lost season, could feel the vibe in and around the stadium, too.

"Electric," said McIntosh. "Absolutely electric. The walk from the locker room down to the field, even at pre-game, was out of control. It was just really, really emotional. It was like no other atmosphere."

Quarterback Brooks Bollinger agreed.

"Anytime we played at 2:30 it was pretty special at Camp Randall," said Bollinger. "But I remember getting out to the field and it was a totally different feel than I've ever been around. In warm-ups there was an absolute electricity. It was one of the most gorgeous days, pretty much the perfect fall day, unseasonably warm. It was one of those 'football was meant to be played that day' types of afternoons, all of the planets aligned, on top of the fact we were going to clinch and go to the Rose Bowl and Ron was going to break the record."

Earlier in the week, Bollinger had a unique realization as to the significance of the moment at hand.

In those days the Badgers were using one of two types of foot-balls – the Wilson 1001 or the Wilson 1005 – during games. The 1005 was a somewhat skinnier ball, making it easier to throw. Wisconsin mostly used the 1001 because of its run-oriented offense and because those balls were easier to kick. It usually took a brand new ball about three weeks to become "game ready." The new balls were hard and slick and they needed to be used to be broken in. Each team brought a dozen or more of their own game balls to a game and, in 1999, student manager Daron Jones was responsible – with Bollinger – for collecting the Badgers' game balls for the coming Saturday's contest.

"We'd do the game balls on Thursday or Friday," said Jones, a native of Deerfield, Wisconsin. "That meant I would go downstairs and rip all the balls out of the different position bags. I would pick out the best 30 or so balls from the 70 or 80 balls we had in those bags. Then Brooks would come along and pick out maybe the best

15. I always wanted to pick out the best ones, but I remember thinking that day that this was going to be something special. We did it on Friday that week and Friday was always a lot more rushed than Thursday. On Thursdays Brooks would come in and we'd joke around or whatever. Fridays they had to get to the hotel so he only had about 15 minutes to do it. I remember us saying that one of the balls was going to be pretty special and Brooks making the comment about making sure we pick out the right one. I remember (placekicker) Vitaly (Pisetsky) would come in and always complain. He'd come and try to pick out the fattest, worst balls he could find because those were the best kicking balls. We always had to put in two really bad balls for Vitaly. Afterward, you realize that's a huge piece of history: the ball that Ron carried to set the NCAA record."

Jones dropped off the Badgers' bag of game balls in the officials' locker room where they checked the air pressure and marked the balls with a line on the last lace as proof they had approved the ball for play that day. Those balls were used only for the game itself, not in warm-ups. Each team's offense used the balls they had selected.

The Badgers and Hawkeyes took the field for warm-ups about an hour and a half before the scheduled 2:36 p.m. kickoff, and the time ticked away toward the 15-minute mark on the scoreboard clock when the UW Marching Band played the National Anthem, followed by a stadium flyover of four F-16s from the Wisconsin Air National Guard's 115th Fighter Wing. It was then time to introduce the senior managers and players from the Badgers' class of 1999. The introductions started with manager Andy Ulery and continued on through a list of players who had become household names to Wisconsin football fans: Ghidorzi. McIntosh. Myers. Pisetsky. Tauscher. Thompson. Dayne was last, but his short walk from the locker room to the north entrance of the stadium was an adventure. UW-Madison police officer Steve

Sasso, who had escorted Dayne at home and on the road for much of the season, recalled fans pushing and pulling at the running back and trying to touch him and grab his jersey. There was security stationed every five feet from the McClain Center exit to the stadium but, according to Sasso, frenzied fans nearly over-ran them. Finally, Dayne appeared at the bottom of the ramp in the north end zone.

Mike Mahnke, the Camp Randall Stadium public address announcer, read from his script as Dayne began to trot from the north end zone out onto the field: "A 5-10, 255-pound running back from Berlin, New Jersey ... greeted by guardians Robbie and Debbie Reid, mother Brenda and father Ron ... the leading candidate for the Heisman Trophy who enters today's game with a chance to become the all-time leading rusher in NCAA history ... number 33, Ron Dayne!"

Dayne made his way toward midfield, but almost forgot to greet the Reids and his parents. "One of the weirdest things for me that day was that I almost ran past my parents," said Dayne, who was obviously caught up in the moment. And it had been a long, often difficult road the family had traveled to reach this remarkable and emotional point in time.

Brenda Reid was the third of 12 children born in Berlin, New Jersey, to Eli and Susie Mae Reid. "My dad's thing was church and school," said Brenda. "You had to go to church and you definitely had to go to school. We could play sports – that was our outlet. I ran track, I played basketball, I played field hockey."

Brenda earned a scholarship to Bluefield State College in Bluefield, West Virginia. She later transferred to Elizabeth City State in Elizabeth City, North Carolina, and upon graduation, she taught for four years before marrying Ron Dayne Sr. and settling in Lynchburg, Virginia. Brenda gave birth there to her first child, Ron, on the afternoon of March 14, 1978. The birth was not without its challenges.

"I went into labor the night of the 13th," Brenda said. "I went into the hospital and they told me that the (umbilical) cord was wrapped around my baby's neck and they kept moving me every five to 10 minutes. They had me hooked up to monitors, but they wouldn't tell me what was wrong. But his godmother had told me that the four fingers on his right hand would save his life and I didn't know what that meant. They didn't give me anything for pain. When he came out, the cord was wrapped around his neck and he had these four fingers in his mouth and he was sucking them. I was just happy that he was here and he was fine. He was seven pounds, 13 ounces, 19 inches long. I got him home – I was scared to leave him with anybody. I was in Virginia and I didn't have any family except for his father's family and I didn't know that many people."

Brenda left her husband when young Ron was 8 years old and moved with her son and 6-year-old daughter, Onya, back to Berlin. Brenda got Ron started playing football again, and he played for a week with other boys who were five and six years older. Brenda then decided that her 8-year-old boy was too young to be playing against teenagers. "I said he had the weight, but he didn't have the maturity," Brenda recalled. "They thought I was joking. They came to the house and they tried to talk to me and I said, 'No, he's eight years old! You've got him playing with boys that are mature and they're built. He's 8; he has that weight on him but he doesn't have that build like he needs."

So young Ron started playing soccer.

"He was almost as big as the coach," Brenda said. "It was two of his cousins that were on the team. They didn't lose a game. The portrait of the team, Ronnie's standing by the coach and he looks like the assistant coach or something."

Brenda's brother, Rob, recalls his nephew's soccer exploits.

"I remember he was so big in comparison to the other kids and, I'm not exaggerating, he kicked the ball for a goal from about the center, where they drop the ball in," Rob Reid said. "The kids kind of parted like the Red Sea, a big kid like him playing among kids … he was always bigger than kids his age. It was just kind of amazing watching him out there playing soccer when he really wanted to play football."

Brenda's young son also ran track, wrestled and played some basketball. He was a top-shelf athlete, regardless of his size.

As Ron grew older, Brenda encountered a variety of difficult issues. She says her ex-husband made repeated attempts to bring young Ron and Onya back to Virginia with him. Her mother was dying of cancer. Eventually Brenda began using drugs.

"It was like anything I could do not to be where I was," Brenda says of her drug use. "Ronnie told me he knew because I stopped painting my fingernails and that was a symbol for him for how to know. And he would say 'Mommy, you alright?' And I'd say, 'Yeah, I'm alright,' but I could see it in his face that he knew I was doing something."

Ron did know and he essentially became the man of the house.

"It was tough," Ron said. "I was probably about 11, maybe, and I found out my mom was doing drugs, so I was like the man of the house from that point on and I had to do everything. I made sure my sister had money for lunch, I had to sign her papers (for school)."

Rob Reid knew something was wrong, too. Brenda worked as a teacher at the correctional facility where Rob also worked. Rob would pick up his sister for work each day and it became clear to him that she was having difficulties.

"She was going through her divorce and stuff like that," Rob Reid said. "She was going through her issues and trying to raise two children and had her own problems, of course. I remember Ron and my oldest son kind of double-teaming me. Ron used to spend weekends at my house when he was still living with his mom. But things had gotten a little difficult for his mother, so he and my oldest son asked me if Ron could come and stay with us. Ron was around the same age; he was a year younger than my oldest son. It was just a natural fit for him to come and live with me and my wife and three other children at that time. We were glad to take Ron in. He was in eighth grade or a freshman in high school at that time. We kind of rallied together as a family."

Ron had only periodic contact with his mother until late in his college career. Onya went to live with her father in Virginia before she eventually returned to New Jersey to live with her uncle, Mark, and his family in the Berlin area. She was able to attend some of her brother's high school games and eventually followed him to the University of Wisconsin. She is now a behavioral care specialist in New Jersey, working with children with psychiatric and behavioral problems.

"It was very difficult for me because I had to be around my mom more than my brother only because I lived in the area where my mom was in the streets running," Onya said. "I would see my mom at her worst. She's better now, but there were plenty of nights where I'd just be worrying, waiting for a phone call telling me they found my mom here or there or whatever. I just prayed for her every night because that's all I could do. Now, it's so much better for my whole family. I'm so happy and I'm so proud of my mom. I knew this time would come when she would be clean, but I just didn't know when it would come. I thank God every day. It's good to have my mom with us and I'm glad she's still alive and breathing and made it through those trials."

Ron's life with his uncle's family was much different from the one he had come from. Rob Reid, like his siblings, was a star athlete. He earned all-state recognition as a high school running back and defensive back and attended Morgan State for a year before transferring to Rowan College, where he set school records for touchdowns and rushing yardage as a three-year starter. He is a member of the school's athletic Hall of Fame.

The 5-7, 160 pound Reid was evaluated and interviewed by several National Football League teams, but he was not drafted, due in part to his size.

"I guess I was kind of disappointed that I wasn't drafted," Reid said. "I felt at that particular time that I was being called in a different direction. So, I completely turned my life around. I had a desire to play football, but not professionally anymore. I believed that God was calling me into the ministry, so I studied under my father, who was a pastor. I went through some courses to become a licensed minister. After being under my father for about two years and graduating from the ministerial requirements, I got called to pastor a little church in Woodbury, a few miles away.

"When I was in college, I had worked part-time for the county. They asked me to come back full-time and I've been here as a civil servant for 34 years. I'm now the minister to a juvenile detention center. I started out as a recreation person, then supervising kids, social worker, went right up the ladder and now the minister of a juvenile detention center."

Reid helped bring discipline and structure to his nephew's life. That was clear to UW assistant coach Bernie Wyatt on a visit to the Reids' home.

"The first time I went to visit him he was at the Reids' home," Wyatt says. "I always tell the story about the first time I went there. I knocked on the door and they answered and I introduced myself – we had talked on the phone, but never met personally – and I said, 'Where's Ron?' They said he was in the kitchen. I went into the kitchen and Ron was in there mopping the kitchen floor. I thought he must be a pretty good kid because there weren't a lot of kids you'd see doing that. It kind of impressed me. That was a good sign."

Ron later showed his appreciation with a letter he wrote to his uncle midway through the 1999 season. Titled "The Heisman," it read:

"I began to think about you and the Heisman Trophy.

"I remember when I first came to live with you and Aunt Deb. The first thing we did was have a family meeting; all of us were sitting around the kitchen table, you, Aunt Deb, Rob Jr., Jaquay and Joel.

"You announced that no one was going to get any new clothes until I had as many outfits as everybody else. Well, Joel did not care about clothes then, Jaquay wore uniforms to school, but Rob got 'swole.' Rob had so many clothes it was ridiculous. And soon after that, I did too. For that Uncle Rob, you win the Heisman.

"I remember you traveling with me on my college visits to Wisconsin and Ohio State. We hated Ohio State, didn't we Uncle Rob? That is why we beat them so badly last week. For traveling with me and helping me make the right decision, you win the Heisman.

"Uncle Rob, you go see Rob play football in Virginia; you go see Jaquay run track in Virginia; but you still come out to Wisconsin to see me, too. For that Uncle Rob, you win the Heisman. And when you do come to Wisconsin, you slip one or two hundred dollar bills in my hand. For that Uncle Rob, YOU REALLY WIN THE HEISMAN.

"When Rob left for college, I started to try some of our tricks by myself, and got caught every time. We never got caught when Rob was home. Like when I squeezed out of the bathroom window one night to see a girl — when I tried to get back in at 1:00 a.m., you had locked that window and the rest of the windows in the house. I had to ring that doorbell and look in your face. You never said a word. You didn't have to. For that Uncle Rob, you win the Heisman.

"Uncle Rob, for never making me feel like a nephew, but always making me feel like a SON, for that Uncle Rob, you win the Heisman."

Standing on the field on Senior Day at Camp Randall Stadium and welcoming the nephew he helped to raise should have been a glorious moment for Rob Reid. Instead it was bittersweet. Earlier that week, Reid says he received a threatening phone call from someone claiming to be a Ricky Williams fan from Texas. The caller told Reid that if his nephew broke the rushing record, "we're going to take him out." Reid was shocked and greatly disturbed.

"I was fortunate and thankful that the university even allowed me to come down (to the field on Senior Day) because his father and mother were there," Reid said. "They really made special recognition and allowed all of us to be down there. It was just great for me. But there were mixed feelings because I had gotten a call from this person from Texas. So, in my mind, I [was thinking] 'Is there somebody in this crowd crazy enough to …?' I was kind of afraid. I had that in my mind. It kind of unnerved me in the midst of such a great record. I guess I had it in the back of my mind and I was kind of on pins and needles, but at the same time I was so thankful that here was a kid that had some difficult hurdles to jump in his life … that he would even be in position to be named with someone like Ricky Williams, to break that record, and that he made the decision to stay in school. I thought 'God has really blessed him.' He didn't really have any injuries that caused him to miss five or six games. It was like a godsend that he was in position to do that. But it was a mixed bag, so to speak, for me."

Once the Senior Day festivities were completed, it was finally game time. Iowa, once the Badgers' yearly nemesis, had hit a low point in its program's history. The Hawkeyes, under first-year head coach Kirk Ferentz (whose staff included linebackers coach Bret Bielema), were rebuilding. Iowa came to Camp Randall Stadium with a defense that ranked 109th nationally against the run and 107th in total defense. The Hawkeyes were 10th or 11th in the Big Ten in run defense, pass efficiency defense, total defense and scoring defense. The all-time series between the two schools was deadlocked (36-36-2) after 74 meetings, but now the Badgers were looking for their third consecutive win over the Hawkeyes.

"We were in very much of a developmental stage as a football team, and our goal was just to go in and do the best we could," Ferentz said. "We didn't have a strong team and I was a little bit concerned in the locker room when it dawned on me that we were starting a walk-on. We had a walk-on named Bart Tolber, who was a linebacker originally; he ended up having to play nose tackle that game for us. Bart was a whopping about 235 and they've got an NFL (offensive) line lined up, so we were focused on doing the best we could. Barry had some excellent football teams up there and I don't know where this one ranks with the other teams that won Rose Bowl games, but from our vantage point, you had just a very veteran, very physical, very, very hard-nosed football team, which I think is vintage Barry Alvarez football. We weren't real thrilled about some of the match-ups — like, basically, all of them — so it was one of those things where we're going to go up there and play our best. It was a mismatch from the start."

The temperature at kickoff was officially listed at 67 degrees, but the thermometer had hit 68 earlier that afternoon. It would eventually hit 69 degrees to break the record of 68 that had been set on November 13, 1909, at the old U.S. Weather Bureau Office at North Hall on the UW campus. The modern-era high temperature record at the Dane County Regional Airport was 67 degrees on November 13, 1989. The 69-degree reading remains a record for that date. The sunny skies and warm temperatures had Badger fans wearing t-shirts and soaking in the "return" of summer.

Iowa won the coin toss and elected to put its offense on the field first. The first three possessions of the game resulted in punts, two by Iowa's Jason Baker and one by the Badgers' Kevin Stemke. As the Hawkeyes were taking possession after Stemke's first punt, Mahnke announced to the crowd inside the stadium that Michigan had defeated Penn State, leaving the Badgers with an opportunity to win the conference title outright and return to the Rose Bowl for the second straight year.

The Badgers' second possession started at their own 20 with

7:49 left in the first quarter and Dayne now needing 95 yards to pass Williams. Bollinger handed to Dayne who proceeded through a huge hole on the left side for a 12-yard gain. Mahnke, true to form, prounounced musically to the crowd: "Rooooonnnnn Daaaayynnne!" And much of the capacity crowd echoed Mahnke's signature call, in unison, right back at him. It was something Mahnke came to enjoy and it brought him a modest bit of popularity around Madison in those days.

Mahnke, who still handles the public address duties at Camp Randall Stadium and the Kohl Center (for Badger men's basketball games), is a 1984 graduate of UW-Madison and started doing P.A. for Badger football and men's basketball games after longtime P.A. man Jack Rane died in 1994. Mahnke believes it was sometime during the 1998 season that the student section in the north end of Camp Randall began repeating his calls after Dayne's runs.

"One of my secrets was that I wouldn't do the full Ron Dayne thing unless he gained seven yards or more, or scored a touchdown," Mahnke once said. "It was kind of cool when that took off (with the fans) and I started having some fun with it late in the 1999 season."

Mahnke's enthusiasm was evident on Dayne's runs, and he did his part to contribute to the tremendous atmosphere inside the stadium, even if that meant following some superstitions.

"I'm a fan in the booth like any fan in the stands, and I get excited when I see something special happen on the field," he said. "Being somewhat superstitious I guess, I drive the same route to the game, make sure I walk the same path, make sure I talk to the same people, get there at exactly two hours before game time. I knew that there was something special happening that night and I didn't want to be the guy who goofed it up by breaking my routine!"

Not everyone enjoyed Mahnke's call, though.

"(Opposing) players would say to me, 'Man, I hate your announcer,' Dayne said. 'All he ever says is Rooonnnn Daaaayyynnne!"

Mahnke could never have known how much his enthusiastic calls after Dayne's long carries had travelled – literally – and helped to connect Wisconsin football fans and alumni in other parts of the country.

More than 900 miles from Madison, in New York City, UW-Madison alumnus Jeffrey Jaffe, accompanied by a friend, had brunch that morning before heading out to find a bar where they could watch the Wisconsin-Iowa game.

"My friend said there was a place around the corner from his apartment," Jaffe said. "He said he didn't even know the name and hadn't been there before and that he didn't even know if there would be Badger fans there. And that was fine with us. We just wanted to go somewhere and watch the game. It was just some little hole-in-the-wall bar. There are thousands of these places in Manhattan. This one just happened to be close.

"We walked in there and it was packed with Badger fans. The whole place was red. From the minute we walked into this place, it was just electric. I remember they had a front section and sort of a back room. The whole place was full of Wisconsin people and it was a pretty young crowd. That neighborhood is popular with people who have just graduated from college or are just moving to the city or have entry level jobs. And I remember the crowd in the bar reflected that demographic, which was good because they were very enthusiastic and really into it. We got a spot at the bar and the game started.

"It was very loud. Every time Dayne got a carry, I remember everyone saying 'Rooooon Daayynnne!' I went to school during the Morton era, so I had never heard that chant. I had flown back for one game, the Michigan game in '97, but Dayne was hurt that day and McCullough played. I never saw Ron play in Madison, so we didn't know that's what they chanted. But it shook the whole bar every time. The other thing I remember is feeling like

Wisconsin's offense was so efficient that [Dayne] might not get enough carries to break the record. I remember Bollinger running quarterback keepers and it seemed like he was looking for someone to tackle him, he had so much room to run."

Indeed, Iowa's defensive strategy entering the game had allowed Bollinger to get free and, in fact, outrush Dayne in the first quarter. Bollinger gained 59 yards on just three attempts in the first period, while Dayne had 10 carries for 37 yards.

"We were overloading the box, trying to do everything we could to stop the run," Bielema said. "I remember Ron didn't have a lot of receiving yards so there were some schemes where we didn't even cover the running back because we didn't see him as a threat in the passing game. We tried to do what we could to take away what Wisconsin did best, which was run the football, but it didn't work very well. There were some [bootlegs] that Brooks was really effective on and they had schemed us a bit on some pressures and he broke loose on one. It was a good job by their coaches to adjust to what we were doing."

Dayne realized Bollinger's value.

"He could run and he could throw," Dayne said. "He was like a little coach out there."

Wisconsin scored on its second drive of the game, completing an eight-play, 80-yard march in 3:51. Bollinger hit fullback Chad Kuhns with a four-yard touchdown pass to put the Badgers ahead 7-0. Iowa went three-and-out on its next possession and the Badgers took over on their own 27. Bollinger and Dayne combined to rush for 46 yards, and Bollinger delivered a 21-yard pass to Kuhns as Wisconsin drove to the Iowa 1-yard line. Dayne scored from there, his 70th career touchdown, and the Badgers led 13-0 after one quarter. Dayne was 62 yards shy of the record.

The Hawkeyes managed a field goal early in the second quarter to cut the Wisconsin lead to 13-3 before the Badgers took over on their own 22 with 9:55 left in the first half, thanks to a 17-yard kickoff return from Nick Davis. A pair of one-yard runs by Dayne and Bollinger, along with a 13-yard gain by Bollinger on third-and-eight, left the Badgers with a first down at their own 37 yard line. On the next play, Bollinger handed to Dayne who again ran through a large hole before making a sharp cut toward the Iowa sideline. Hawkeye defensive back Shane Hall, trying to get back into position after Dayne's cut, was left in the unenviable position of having to arm-tackle the Badger running back. He could not hang on, and Dayne headed downfield for a 37-yard gain. ABC play-by-play man Tim Brandt correctly stated, "No one arm tackles this guy."

Dayne was 23 yards from the record, but it would have to wait a little longer. Bollinger finished the drive by tossing a 24-yard touchdown pass to wide receiver Chris Chambers for a 20-3 Wisconsin lead. The scenarios that UW athletic officials had hoped would develop during the week were coming together as if they had been scripted to do so. The weather was more typical of Madison in June than in November. Penn State had lost. The Badgers were easily handling the Hawkeyes. Only one scenario remained to be played out, and everyone was doing the math.

The Atmospheric, Oceanic and Space Science Building on the UW-Madison campus, standing 16 stories tall (plus a penthouse), is located just a few blocks east of Camp Randall Stadium at the corner of Dayton and Orchard Streets. Though the building was clearly visible from inside the west side of Camp Randall Stadium in 1999, it normally has nothing to with Badger football home games. But this was, of course, not a normal circumstance. Dave Santek and Russ Dengel, a pair of researchers who worked in the building, decided they would take part in Dayne's final push toward Williams' record by displaying the yardage he need-ed on the penthouse of the building. They called it the Dayne-Meter.

"It almost started out as a joke," Dengell said. "We couldn't get into the game – it was sold out – and we were sitting in Dave's office and we said we should do something. At first, we thought we should have big numbers that hang off the side of the building or something like that. Well, that was just ridiculous because we never could've done that. So then we said we could make littler numbers and it sort of snowballed from there."

They brought a television, a radio and a grill for bratwurst up to the roof of the building.

"We had this special printer/plotter that's probably three or four feet wide and it's just on a big roll so we were able to print out large numbers," Santek said. "And we were trying to remember how tall these numbers were – I was thinking probably 10 to 12 feet high. The countdown started at 99, so we just had two sets of each number and then we had them fixed on something to give them some kind of a backing. It might have been cardboard or wood frame or something big and stable so we could hang them up and pull them down."

Santek and Dengell continued to switch out the numbers, with some help from the Camp Randall crowd, as Dayne barreled toward the record. They kept track of his yardage by watching television and listening to Matt Lepay's local radio call.

"The crowd was just amazing because when Dayne was [gaining] some of the short yardage, when they kept handing the ball off to him several times, we couldn't keep up with the numbers so we just kind of waited until there was a break," Santek said. "The crowd was encouraging us to change the number because we weren't up to date. But [it was] really loud."

When Dayne and the Badger offense took the field with 4:40 left in the second quarter, the Dayne-Meter showed 23 yards to go.

Luke Behnke and the rest of the student section inside the stadium were also counting down.

"They didn't have [the video scoreboard] then," Behnke said. "They had that very simple lighted board across from the student section. I remember they had put up how many yards he had left. They would update it periodically, so we would all do the math, saying 'Okay, he's 43 yards away, he's 23 yards away ...' I remember everyone was so focused on it."

Glenn Betts was doing the math, too. In fact, he had been doing it the entire season. The UW athletic department had an apparel agreement with Reebok at the time, and Reebok had agreed to sponsor a billboard on the outside south wall of the UW Field House. The billboard displayed a large, white number 33, along with the phrase "Running for the Record." Below that phrase was the yardage total Dayne needed to reach Williams' record. Betts, a member of the UW athletics maintenance staff, was charged with climbing a ladder each week and changing the number. Betts knew the number needed to be changed to zero once Dayne got there. Betts was assisting with the conversion of the Field House to prepare for a Badger volleyball match, but he had heard Dayne was getting close so he headed into the stadium to have a look.

They were also keeping close track of Dayne's yardage where it mattered most: in the press box. Bill Mott, the son of the late former UW sports information director Jim Mott, has for years been the person who "spots the ball" from a statistical standpoint for the Badger sports information staff. Sports information director Steve Malchow was in constant contact with not only Mott, but also Patrick Herb, then a student assistant in the UW sports information office, who was serving as a sideline liaison to Malchow. Malchow kept Herb informed of Dayne's progress so the Badger sideline was updated, and he was in contact with ABC, which was frequently displaying for its viewers the number of yards that Dayne needed.

"Every play he had the ball, I was making sure of the right amount of rushing yards he had," said Jon Corl, the ABC graphics man. "That was my role for the day, making sure that I was right, and that when he broke the record, it broke (on the TV screen) at the right time. The good part about that for me was that it was clear he just broke it. It wasn't 'did he get the two yards or didn't he?' For me, personally, he helped me do my job correctly. I owe him a beer or a sandwich or something for not being in a position of wondering whether he broke it or not. So I didn't get heat from my producer for getting it wrong and I didn't convey to the world that he just broke the record when he didn't. Back in the day, Rudy Martzke of *USA Today* used to have his column where he'd have, for example, the 'graphics screw-up of the day' or something."

Dayne made sure there would be no doubt about whether or not he broke the record. The Badgers took over at their own 17-yard line with 4:40 remaining in the second quarter. They led 20-3. Bollinger took the snap from Casey Rabach, turned to his left and handed the ball to Dayne five yards behind the line of scrimmage. Dayne headed slightly to the right and through a hole created by blocks from Dave Costa and Mark Tauscher. He crossed the 23-yard line with Hall, the Iowa defensive back, right in front of him. But Dayne gave Hall a little fake and the Hawkeye defender was left to watch Dayne run right by him. Dayne then got out into the open behind Chambers who was taking aim at Iowa defensive back Joe Slattery. Dayne, however, didn't use the Chambers block. Instead he ran between Chambers and Slattery, even knocking Chambers down in the process. He didn't stop until Tarig Holman brought him down 31 yards later at the Badger 48-yard line. "Open up the history books," ABC's Brandt proclaimed. "Here comes Ron Dayne!" Matt Lepay, the Badgers' longtime radio play-by-play man, told his audience,simply, "Ron Dayne has become the NCAA's all-time career rushing leader!"

Camp Randall Stadium was up for grabs. Wide receiver Nick Davis was the first of Dayne's teammates to reach him, and Davis bounced up and down, slapping Dayne's helmet. Kuhns was next and he was followed by a host of Badgers, all of whom wanted to congratulate the new all-time rushing king. The moment touched people in so many different ways.

"When he got that ball and he came right down our side, I felt like I was running with him and when he rolled and came back up, I said 'it's over,'" recalled Dayne's mother, Brenda, who was holding off a television interview right before her son's famous run. "Everybody was cheering, and I felt like I wanted to kiss everybody but I was trying to help the camera man up off the ground. He was stuck between the seats – he was down and the camera was [pointing] up in the air and we had to help the camera man get up. He was trying to talk to us and we said, 'We can't because he's getting ready to break this record.' When Ronnie started running, everybody was jumping and cheering and by the time he fell, he rolled and he came back up, stood up and everybody was cheering and saying, 'Where's the (camera) guy?'"

But Brenda was happy for her son, who had finally proven all the doubters wrong once and for all. "In any sport that Ronnie played, it was always something he had to do to prove to people that he could do what they thought he couldn't do," Brenda said.

In the press box, Malchow and his staff confirmed what everyone already could see.

"I remember when he made the carry, because the carry that broke the record was pretty long," Malchow said. "I think we all knew it and yet we kind of all were looking at Bill Mott, as I recall, who was probably keeping the stats manually, and he was nodding his head and I'm waving at Kevin Kluender and Mike Mahnke down in the P.A. booth and it was like chain reaction stuff. It had to start somewhere, somebody saying, 'Yeah, it's officially the record' and then it all started lining up as we hoped it would."

The Dayne-Meter went to zero and so did the billboard on the outside of the Field House.

"Everybody was jumping up and down and celebrating and I thought, 'I should go change the sign,' Betts said. "There wasn't anyone nearby that I could grab to help me, so immediately I walked to the other end of the Field House and picked up the ladder (a ladder was staged at the south end of Field House for that purpose). Usually I had someone holding the ladder for me, but that day there wasn't anyone around so I did it myself because I knew they wanted the sign changed. It was kind of eerie because there was so much excitement in the stadium but on the south end of the Field House it was pretty quiet. But I thought it was kind of nice, there was no one there to bother me. As I was just starting to put up the zero, somebody yelled from below, 'Can I take your picture?' I looked down and there was a photographer down there and he actually took my picture while I was changing the number to zero. It ended up in the paper the next day. My parents actually bought the picture and had it framed for me. That was neat. It was one of my highlights of working at UW."

Inside the Field House, on the east side, was a satellite branch of the UW Bookstore. It had made available roughly 1,500 t-shirts that said "All-time Rushing Leader" on them. Once Dayne broke the record, the shirts were gone in less than 25 minutes.

Brian Ebner, a photographer shooting that day for *The Capital Times,* had moved from the south end zone to the west sideline, just north of the Badgers' bench area where he thought he might have a good shot of Dayne. He ended up capturing Dayne from the side on the record run. Digital photo transmission had not taken hold yet, so someone had to physically take Ebner's film back to get it developed. *The Capital Times* essentially started printing an "extra" around halftime, and by the end of the game, they were being sold outside the stadium. Ebner's photo was on the front page.

"If it wouldn't have happened that play, and if I wouldn't have been able to make it up to the other side of the bench, I would have completely missed it," Ebner said. "To me, I thought it was a huge chance. In hindsight, I don't know if I would have done the same thing. But I'm really glad I did."

The record run, of course, meant so much to Dayne's teammates who had worked hard to help him catch Williams and felt a part of the accomplishment, just as Alvarez had told them they would prior to the start of the season.

"When he made that (record) run, he actually ran me over," said Chambers. "I got run over for the record. I was blocking for him and he totally ran me over. When you're blocking for Ron, you cannot look back, as a receiver, and watch him do his thing. Our whole goal was to stay in front of our man and let the running back cut off. I guess I got in his way and he decided to run me over and I kind of rolled over and watched him run from there. But that's the way it went down and I have no problem with it. It's the memory of a lifetime for me."

Nick Davis had made a special effort to improve his downfield blocking skills, knowing that he might be able to help spring a long run if he did his job well.

"The way the coaches and everybody were talking about it, it was an individual achievement but it was a team effort," Davis said of Dayne's run at the record. "Going into that season, that's one thing I really worked on because I wasn't the best blocker. I had the talent and physical strength to be a good blocker and the coaches saw that and got on me about it. I made a concerted effort to do that. I remember being so happy for him, not only because I consider Ron a great friend and teammate, but it was a team effort as well. It was like scoring a touchdown, that's how excited I was at the moment."

Chad Kuhns had spent the entire season lining up in front of Dayne as the Badgers' starting fullback, but the two were not in the game together much on the series prior to the record run.

"One thing that really stood with me on that day was Chad,"

Dayne said. "Chad was like 'just don't break the record without me — I gotta be in the game!' I started laughing and I said, 'How many yards do I need?' and he's like, 'Don't break the record without me.' Then I had that long run and [the coaches] kept him in and we did it."

Kuhns did, indeed, want to be on the field when the historic moment occurred.

"I knew he was getting close," Kuhns said. "He came off the field and I was on the field because there was a one back set play. I talked to him afterward and said, 'Don't break the record without me — wait till I get back in there.' The very next play that I got in, I believe the play was a 23 Zone, and I just wanted to make sure I made the best possible block I could to make sure he breaks the record. I remember blocking my guy and my guy fell to the ground and I fell on top of him and I looked up and I saw Ron running and I thought that should be enough to get it. I was just excited to get up and run down and jump on him and get excited for him that he broke the record."

Dayne's record may have meant more to the Badgers' offensive linemen than any other group of people connected with the program. They were the ones who toiled, game after game, fighting it out in the trenches and battling to open holes through which Dayne could run.

"The offensive linemen, we loved to eat and we ate at Mickie's quite a bit," said guard Bill Ferrario, referring to the well-known Madison diner across the street from Camp Randall Stadium and the UW Field House. "Each week we'd go there and I remember [the Reebok billboard] on the front of the Field House, the yardage decreasing each week to show how many Ron needed to break the record. I remember being at Mickie's the week of the Iowa game. I think it was me and Costa and, maybe, Rabach, and looking up and seeing that number and knowing that it was attainable and just thinking we needed to get that many yards and we'll have blocked for the running back that's rushed for more yards than anyone in college football history."

It was ironic, then, that Ferrario – responsible for helping Dayne accumulate so much of his yardage – was not on the field for the record-breaking run. Ferrario, who would go on to become just the third player in Big Ten history to start 50 games, had sprained his ankle the week before in the fourth quarter at Purdue.

"So, the next week was the first week that I truly ever missed even a practice," Ferrario said. "Coach Hueber told me that I was going to start the game against Iowa. We all knew the record was on the line that game and we all knew before the game started how many yards Ron needed. For me, take away the record, I just didn't want to not be on the field. Just as a pride issue, I didn't want to be out of the game, let alone all the other stuff. Hueber told me I was going to start the game, but he stressed to me that if he saw me hobble on it at all or not get my job done at all, that I was going to be coming out. So I was nervous going into the game knowing Ron's record was on the line and that my ankle was extremely bad going into it. The series before Ron broke the record – I was basically hobbling the whole start of the game – Hueber said I was going to be benched for a series, get [the ankle] taped and he'd re-evaluate me."

Fifth-year senior Rob Roell replaced Ferrario in the lineup at left guard. Roell, who had started twice during his career, was an important reserve for the Badgers, able to play guard or center. In many ways he was like a valuable "sixth man" in basketball. He was not a starter, but he saw plenty of action throughout his career, spelling Rabach or one of the guards in a variety of situations. Roell believed he would play against the Hawkeyes because it was Senior Day and because it was not uncommon for him to see significant playing time. He was in the game when Dayne broke the record, but he injured his knee when the Badgers scored later in the drive and didn't return to action that day.

"You do [feel bad for Ferrario] because he had invested so much time into it," said Jim Hueber, the team's offensive line coach. "But the thing that can't get lost in the fact that he broke that record was that we needed to win that game. There wasn't going to be any compromise because, somewhere along the line, that play was going to happen. There wasn't going to be any compromise with the fact that we had to win that game.

"Rob had jumped in there and played for us a couple different times during the season for somebody that needed a rest or to fill in or something like that, but there was no underlying factor as to why [Ferrario] wouldn't have been in there except I probably just didn't feel like he could get it done. And then you look at him at the end of the game and everybody else was in there, and you knew what he had done to get us to that point.

"There's no question Rob played a bunch for us in a backup role. If Billy was out of the game, it was either I felt like [his ankle] was bothering him or I felt like he needed a rest. But, again, there was no way you would know what particular play it would be that he would hit it on. That's fate and everyone is going to have a different memory of that."

Ferrario initially felt some disappointment at not being on the field when Dayne broke the record, but he holds no resentment.

"Long story short, I wasn't keeping track of the record, Hueber wasn't keeping track of the record and, next thing you know, I've got my ankle taped up and Ron breaks the record on the field," Ferrario said. "For the moment, I was a little disappointed, but I said to [Coach Hueber] afterward that I didn't expect him to keep track. Like everybody else on that team, I wanted what was best for the team. I wanted to win, I wanted our team to be successful, so I held no ill will about it.

"I think it was tough for a minute because nobody was standing on the sidelines saying, 'Okay, he's got 20 yards, okay he's got 30 yards.' Our ultimate goal at the time was to win the game. Coach Alvarez was criticized at times for not leaving Ron in during the fourth quarters of games we were winning, but between the coaching staff and players, our first and foremost goal was to win games. For a quick minute I was a little disappointed that I wasn't a part of [the record run], but at the same time I realized it gave [an opportunity to] Rob Roell, who had busted his butt on that offensive line in a backup role. I feel horrible Rob hurt his knee on that play at the end of that series, but maybe that was a part of fate for him that he got to be in on that play. He can always say, 'I didn't start at Wisconsin, but I was in on the play when Ron Dayne broke the record.'"

What is clear in the voices of Ferrario and Roell is that they both badly wanted to be on the field and be a part of the team effort to not only help Dayne break Williams' record, but also to help the Badgers win the conference title. Roell could have been speaking for the entire offensive line when he expressed his appreciation for Dayne.

"Every offensive lineman wants to block for a great running back and every running back wants a great offensive line," Roell said. "I personally take a lot of pride in being one of the offensive linemen that helped him get to where he got. I take as much pride in that as being part of the championship teams. What was great about [Dayne] is that he was not an arrogant guy. He knew he was good, but he would always give the offensive line credit when he was speaking to the press or when he was accepting awards. I don't believe there was one time where he didn't give the offensive line credit. He was a real stand-up guy as far as that went."

If there was a signature Ron Dayne run, this might have been it. It was, of course, the record run, but it also was a run that tied together all the elements Dayne brought to the table as a running back.

"That was a typical Ronnie run," Alvarez said. "It was a patient run. He ran through some tackles, some people rubbed off of him and he comes off on the other side of it. It was a combination of everything: his patience, his vision, his size where people just bounce off of him, he ran through some stuff and used his speed to pull way from people."

Dayne got up off the turf after being tackled and was mobbed by his teammates. Pat Richter, then the UW Director of Athletics, knew the ball Dayne carried on the record play would be apt to somehow disappear and was aware enough to keep track of the ball. It ended up in Dayne's hands and, as he started back toward the Badgers' huddle for the next play, he tossed the ball to assistant coach Bernie Wyatt, the man who had recruited him five years earlier and become a trusted friend and advisor.

"When Ronnie broke the record, he came over to the sideline and flipped me the ball," Wyatt said. "I didn't think anything of it, you know? I held onto it for him and after the game I said, 'Ron, here's the ball.' He said, 'No, I want you to have it.' I still have it. John Chadima got it all printed up for me. One of these days I'll give it back to the university. Ron was that way. All the awards and all were important, but he never got blown out of the water about it. He was kind of a shy, low-key guy."

Henry Mason, who was in charge of the Wisconsin wide receivers, recalls watching the run from the sideline. He took in the moment, but also realized there was a game to finish.

"As I watch it, I know what the play is and I know that Chris' assignment is going to require some thinking on his part as to who to block," Mason said. "My first thought was, 'Okay, he blocked the right guy.' Then my eyes flashed back to Ron and he starts breaking through and I thought, 'Chris, you've got a good block going here, just hold on, just hold the block.' Lo and behold, [Ron] runs right up Chris's back and knocks him over. I always tease Chris that Ron's run would have been longer if he'd been out of the way.

He got tackled maybe five yards past me. You realize he has enough, that he just broke it. The crowd started going nuts. That span of two or three seconds seemed to last a minute and you could really get into it. Then all of a sudden you're right back into it, what we had to get done."

In the huddle, the Badger players, too, realized there was still more than half a game left to play.

"When Ron broke that record, the place just erupted," said Casey Rabach. "I remember standing in the huddle looking at the other linemen and it was just kind of a relief for Ron to get that record. It was done and over with and now it was 'let's go finish and win this game.'"

There was just one problem with Rabach's plan.

"I remember getting really excited about [the record run] and the game stopped for a couple minutes," Nick Davis said. "Then we got back into the huddle and Brooks kind of brought every-body back together and was talking about what we needed to do and Chris McIntosh said 'We've got a game to play now.' I remember breaking the huddle and Chris (Chambers) and I were going to the wide side of the field and all of a sudden the naked guy runs like three feet in front of me. I didn't even see him and I turned around and there's a naked guy running down the field. I remember looking at Chris Chambers and laughing and him just shaking his head and laughing."

Thousands who were at that game remember the infamous streaker, who ran the length of the field from north to south right after Dayne's run that broke Williams' record.

Tim Condon was a sophomore at UW-Madison in the fall of 1999. A native of Sullivan, Wisconsin, he had begun his college career intent on studying engineering, but soon became more interested in communications-related work and, in fact, began working for Wisconsin Public Television. Condon lived with sev-eral friends in a house on Main Street. One night, as he and his friends discussed their plans for the coming school year, the subject of Dayne's run at Williams' record arose.

"And that's when I came up with the idea," Condon said. "If he's going to do this, someone needs to do something for this game. I might as well streak across the field! And that was the end of it – it was a mere mention, we didn't really talk about it. My friends all laughed and said, 'Oh yeah, that's great! If anyone's going to do it, you should do it!'"

One of Condon's roommates had "dressed up" as a streaker for Halloween that fall, so Condon had a trench coat if he needed one. He woke up on the morning of the Wisconsin-Iowa game and went to lunch with one of his roommates, who reminded him of his idea about running naked across the field at Camp Randall.

"I had remembered I said that, but until that day, several hours before the game, I didn't put any thought into it," Condon said. "We pretty much shook hands at the end of that meal – he was going to work that day at a restaurant – and he said, 'When I leave work today, I want to know you've done this.' And so then it was me just by myself walking down State Street and I'm saying, 'Am I really going to do this?'

"Well of course, me, I call my mom just to let her know there's a potential I might be getting in trouble and I might need to get bailed out of jail. Being the great parent that she was and still is, she just laughed. I'd been in trouble in high school – nothing serious, but pulled a lot of pranks. Anyway, she said, 'Make sure you're not drinking because you don't want to get a drinking ticket out of it.' And I knew that if I was to be drinking that day, that was how the story was going to go: 'drunk kid gets in trouble for running across the football field naked.' I just didn't want to add that extra trouble; I knew I was going to get in trouble anyway. All she said was don't get in trouble for drinking, don't get kicked out of school, and, in her words, don't damage your manhood, if you know what I mean. My original idea was to run around on the field, do a U-turn and just jump back into the stands and be hidden underneath my trench coat. Why I thought I was going to be able to accomplish that, I don't know."

Condon eventually headed to a pre-game party where he began telling others what he was planning to do at the game and why he was not drinking. He was sitting in Section M in the north end of the stadium, wearing nothing but a pair of mesh shorts under the trench coat, as Dayne neared the record on the second-quarter drive that ended with Bollinger's 24-yard touchdown pass to Chris Chambers. Condon had actually made his way down to the field level and was ready to go when Bollinger and Chambers connected. Some of the students around him knew what he was going to do.

"A few of them knew," Condon said. "But I was already standing by the field and ready to go during that drive and, after the drive was over, I was like, 'Okay, I can't just continue to stand here, I have to go back up to my seat.' So I go back up to my seat, and those who didn't know what I was doing started asking questions. 'Hey, guy in the trench coat, what are you doing?' Actually it really got weird when I had these mesh shorts on underneath, and I knew that my original intention was just to take them off by the field and go for it. But I knew I wasn't going to have time, plus I was shaking at this point. Anyway I'm in the stands and I take my shorts off and these girls were sitting by me and they're like, 'What are you doing?!' So then, full disclosure to not be the creeper before they call the police over, I'm like, 'No, no, no! This is what I'm going to do!' And that's when everyone heard it. And at this point there are just hundreds of people in the stands who know what's going to happen, and there's no turning back at this point, if I was even considering turning back."

The Badgers began to gather in their huddle after Dayne's historic run and that's when Condon made his. He was wearing a red bandana, white socks, tennis shoes and nothing more. Condon had painted his face white with a red W on each cheek. A large number 33 – with Dayne's name above it – was painted on his torso. And a pair of red Ws adorned his backside. He ran down the field, heading toward the south end zone, arms in the air and a big smile on his face. He even stopped briefly at the 20-yard line to strike a "Heisman pose." He finished his run and then calmly walked the last few steps toward waiting police officers underneath the goal post. The officers handcuffed him, wrapped him up and took him from the playing field.

"They were pretty upset," Condon said of the police officers. "I remember they asked me who I was, and one of them said, 'So you were a student here, huh?' And I'm like, 'No, I AM a student here!' And they said, 'Well, you're not going to be after this.' And I got a little bit scared for a second. Still, all I could do at this point was just focus my eyes on the crowd and people were just so uproarious about it. I loved it."

WHA-TV, the Madison affiliate of Wisconsin Public Television where Condon was employed, was doing the game for its customary tape-delay telecast later that night. Deb Piper was in the WHA production truck.

"At that time, we were on a shot of the coaches' booth," Piper said. "You could tell they were watching the streaker because they were looking to their right and chuckling and smiling, so you know they had seen it as well. It was funny to see on our monitor and then to find out a couple weeks later that the kid who did the streaking was actually on our production crew but was not working for us that day. He had been newly hired and was in the student section as a fan, but we found out that we had that connection and he was on our crew. It was hysterical."

Condon was charged with lewd and lascivious behavior, unlawful entry to the playing field and disorderly conduct. He had spent a couple hours in a jail cell downtown when he was informed that he had some visitors.

"It was all those roommates that I was living with in that house, along with the kid that I told I was going to do it earlier in the day, along with a couple other friends," Condon said. "I just assumed that they were going to collect money to get me out of jail because my bail was roughly $1,000. That was not at all the case. I see them and I'm like, 'So, you guys got the money?' And they said, 'No, we just wanted to come see you in jail!' So I had them get my wallet and I ended up charging myself out of jail that day."

Condon, who now works for an investment company in Arizona, ended up having all charges dropped after he completed 60 community service hours working at Wisconsin Public Television. Dayne recalls Condon visiting him at his apartment the night of the Wisconsin-Iowa game, but Condon believes they first met, by chance, in the parking lot of a Madison video store. Either way, Condon's message to Dayne was that he had not intended to upstage the running back's big day.

"I did eventually talk to him about it, but it was in the parking lot of Blockbuster Video," Condon said. "He was returning a video and I was like, 'Hey, I just wanted you to know that I'm that guy.' I was really apologetic. I said, 'Just so you know, I wasn't trying to take away anything that happened that day; it was just me doing my thing. It was a really awesome day.' That's all the words we exchanged. And he was like, 'No, I think it's cool! I think it's great!' So what more can you ask for? Really, that's all I wanted to say. I wanted him to know that I wasn't a weirdo, basically. I wasn't some kind of stalking super-fan; I was just caught up in the moment."

Dayne had finally set the record that had been on the minds of the Badgers and their fans for so long. It was the last scenario necessary to make it a perfect afternoon. It was inconceivable that the day could become more special than it already was. But it did.

As Bollinger guided the Badgers down the field after Dayne's run and hit Chambers with a 16-yard touchdown pass with 1:18 left in the first half, Brandt told those watching on television, "Ron Dayne has just run himself into the College Football Hall of Fame in South Bend, Indiana; he's just become the leading all-time rusher; and he's just wrapped up the Heisman."

Wisconsin led 27-3 at halftime. The Badgers were dominating in all phases of the game, outgaining the Hawkeyes, 340-126, in total yardage and holding a six-minute edge in time of possession. Dayne had 127 yards and a touchdown on 17 carries. Bollinger was having a brilliant afternoon, completing 7-of-8 passes for 115 yards and three scores, and running for 96 yards on just eight attempts.

The Badgers began the second half by marching 74 yards in six plays to the Iowa 1-yard line. Dayne had his longest run of the day – 38 yards – on the drive, but the Hawkeyes put together a goal-line stand that halted Dayne twice and Bollinger once. Wisconsin turned the ball over on downs. Iowa went three-and-out on its ensuing series and the Badgers scored the next time they had the ball, with Bollinger running for a 2-yard touchdown to give Wisconsin a 34-3 lead with 4:55 left in the third quarter. The Hawkeyes failed to convert on fourth down from the Badgers' 33-yard line on their next possession and Wisconsin took over with 1:42 remaining in the third period.

Dayne ran to the right side for seven yards on first down, before heading to the left on his next carry, a 10-yard gain that put him over 200 yards for the afternoon. Dayne joined Williams and USC legend Marcus Allen as the only players in NCAA Division I history to register 11 200-yard rushing performances. Then, with 51 seconds left in the third quarter, Bollinger handed the ball to Dayne on first and 10 from midfield. Dayne bulled his way up the middle for 13 more yards as Mahnke enthusiastically proclaimed, "Roooonnnnn Daaaaayyynnne!" The entire stadium echoed Mahnke's call and that was it. McIntosh, the lineman with whom Dayne had played the longest, helped him up and Dayne headed for the Wisconsin sideline, giving the crowd a few pumps of the fist with his right arm. Dayne's playing career in Camp Randall Stadium was over, as Alvarez, true to form, pulled him out of the game late in the third quarter of a one-sided victory just as he had done numerous times before. Dayne finished with 216 yards and a touchdown on 27 carries for an average of 8.0 yards per attempt.

Bollinger left the game early in the fourth quarter. He had put together a remarkable afternoon, rushing for 113 yards and a touchdown on only 11 carries, while completing 9 of 12 passes for 144 yards and three scores. He and Dayne would end up combining to account for 473 of Wisconsin's 604 yards of total offense that day.

Bollinger gave way to Scott Kavanagh, the senior whose starting job the redshirt freshman had taken five weeks into the season. Kavanagh was joined by Dayne's backup, Eddie Faulkner, in the backfield and the pair guided the Badgers to the Iowa 1-yard line. Facing fourth and goal, Kavanagh took the snap, turned to his right, faked a handoff to Faulkner, reversed direction and scored on a bootleg into the left side of the end zone. There were few who didn't feel good seeing Kavanagh score. He had shown maturity and senior leadership despite his diminished role on the field. He has special memories of the 1999 Iowa game.

"It was awesome," Kavanagh recalled. "If you're just a football fan and there was a perfect football day you could put together from start to finish,that was probably it. The atmosphere ... even on Friday, on campus, there was a buzz about the whole thing.

"One thing that stands out to me was it was Senior Day and I got out to my parents (during the pre-game ceremony) and I looked at my dad and he was crying. I'd never seen my dad cry before. He's old-school, grew up on the south side of Chicago. He said to me, 'So, this is what it's like for you guys.' And I said, 'Well, it's not like this ALL the time.' For me that was a major

The Wisconsin sideline began to erupt during Ron Dayne's NCAA

Tim Condon – "The Streaker" – is escorted away from the playing field by police after his run from one end of the field to the other. He was wearing only a bandana and tennis shoes. (Photo courtesy of Mike DeVries)

Thousands of Badger fans saluted Ron Dayne by holding up white commemorative towels in a spontaneous show of appreciation after the 1999 win over Iowa. (Photo Courtesy of Mike DeVries)

Dayne and his parents are all smiles on Senior Day at Camp Randall Stadium in 1999. Dayne broke the NCAA rushing record later that day. (Photo Courtesy of UW Athletic Communications)

Badger fans were swept up in Dayne's run at the NCAA rushing record as well as letting some Iowa fans know who was going to win the Heisman Trophy. (Photo courtesy of Mike DeVries)

Ron Dayne (4) as a youth football player. (Photos Courtesy of Ron Dayne)

The countdown to Dayne's run at Ricky Williams' rushing record included the "Dayne-meter" that was displayed during the 1999 Iowa game high atop the UW's Atmospheric and Oceanic Sciences Building just east of Camp Randall Stadium. (Photo Courtesy of Dannielle Dirienzo)

record-setting run. (Photo courtesy of Mike DeVries)

Dayne was engulfed by media on the field after breaking the NCAA rushing record against Iowa. (Photo Courtesy of UW Athletic Communications)

Ron Dayne, Chris McIntosh, Barry Alvarez and Pat Richter share smiles as they look out over the crowd assembled during the postgame celebration. (Photo courtesy of Mike DeVries)

Surrounded by teammates, coaches, media and the UW Band, Dayne addresses the Camp Randall Stadium crowd after his record-setting day. (Photo courtesy of Dannielle Dirienzo)

Heisman Trophy finalists: Drew Brees (Purdue), Joe Hamilton (Georgia Tech), Ron Dayne (Wisconsin), Michael Vick (Virginia Tech) and Chad Pennington (Marshall). (Photo courtesy of AP/Heisman Trophy Trust)

Ron Dayne, with his recently won Heisman Trophy in the foreground, gives his acceptance speech at the Downtown Athletic Club's black-tie affair. (Photo courtesy of AP/Heisman Trophy Trust)

Nearly eight years to the day he broke the NCAA rushing record, Dayne and his family joined Barry Alvarez on the field at Camp Randall Stadium as Dayne's number was officially retired by the UW at halftime of the 2007 Michigan game. (Photo Courtesy of UW Athletic Communications)

memory of that day. Something like that is a lot more memorable or important to me than scoring a touchdown. I'll never forget that. We later got the picture of us and my parents have it hanging up in their house. To be able to share something like that with your parents, that was nice."

The Hawkeyes responded with a lengthy 70-yard drive that ended when Badger defensive lineman Wendell Bryant recovered a fumble by Iowa quarterback Scott Mullen at the Wisconsin nine-yard line. During that drive, the Badgers welcomed a surprise visitor to their sideline. Alvarez had been coaching from the press box for weeks due to his ailing knee, but he wanted to be down on the field with his players and he had arranged to move down once the game was in hand. John Chadima, then an administrative assistant for the football program, went up to get Alvarez early in the fourth quarter.

"I actually drove him from the backside of the press box around the north side of the stadium down the north tunnel," said Chadima. "That was the first time he had come on the field since the Cincinnati game that year. I got goose bumps. I remember people seeing him as we were driving and just going nuts. I took a golf cart and it was dead on Breese Terrace, there was nobody there. We had a special railing installed on the steps leading up from Breese Terrace – it's still there and Joe Paterno used it when Penn State played here in 2008. We stopped kind of behind the goal post and he got out and walked and that's when people started to recognize him."

Alvarez made his way from the back of the north end zone to the Wisconsin sideline as the crowd cheered and chanted his name. He was greeted by smiling staff members and players. Rabach, Costa and Ferrario were the first three players to hug Alvarez and they were followed by Pisetsky and Tauscher. Then, in front of Alvarez, stood Dayne. The coach and the soon-to-be Heisman Trophy winner embraced – just as they had when Alvarez first met

Dayne on his recruiting visit to Wisconsin – and shared a special moment for the two of them and for the entire program and its followers. Dayne had largely helped to define Wisconsin football during the Alvarez era.

"I always thought – and I may have said it when he broke the record – he was the symbol of what Barry Alvarez was trying to build," said Matt Lepay. "A guy who had power. A guy who would find ways to win. And a guy who didn't have a lot to say. That, to me, was what Barry's guys were about. You play the game. You're physical, you're tough, you may not be overly sexy, but you're very effective. And you don't spend a lot of time worrying about being glib in an interview setting. I thought that was Dayne and, to a large extent, what the program was under Barry."

Temperatures had dropped only slightly, into the lower 60s, and darkness had fallen on Madison by the time Wisconsin took over at its own 9-yard line with 7:21 remaining. The Badgers simply needed to milk the clock and run out the remaining minutes of the game before the party could officially get started, and they did that primarily by handing the ball to a little-known running back whose name didn't even appear on the team's "three-deep" depth chart.

Matt Unertl, who had initially attended UW-LaCrosse before becoming a walk-on for the Badgers in 1997, entered the game in the fourth quarter once Dayne, Bennett and Faulkner had done their work for the day. Unertl gained 37 yards on seven carries as the Badgers moved to the Iowa six-yard line. Mahnke, of course, called out Unertl's name on each carry and, as he did so, the student section in the north end of the stadium echoed the backup running back's name, Ron Dayne-style. As the Badgers approached the end zone, the students were rhythmically chanting "Matt U-ner-tl, Matt U-ner-tl" even between plays. The scene was an expression of the spontaneity, pure joy and penchant for fun that was so evident in Camp Randall that day.

"Matt's cousin actually lived on my dorm floor and he had told me how much [Matt] appreciated that chant," said Luke Behnke. "He'd come in and do the workhorse stuff at the end of the game once the game was put out of reach and that was pretty fun to continue that tradition with Matt. It didn't go on much after that. I thought for years to come that every running back would get that kind of a thing, but maybe the names didn't work so well. It kind of died out."

For Unertl, it was an unexpected happening, but something he cherishes.

"After that first carry, people were doing the "Matt Unertl" thing," he said. "At first it wasn't as loud, but then once we got down to the 20- or 30-yard-line, I was in the huddle with my head down and [teammates] were hitting me on the shoulders and they're like, 'You hear that?' I realized people were saying it back-to-back and not even when I was carrying the ball. Then they were just chanting 'Matt Unertl!' For Ron it was different because he was starting and used to being in there, but for them to just start doing it and for the amount of people that started doing it, I guess it was just kind of crazy. I guess it was a little overwhelming – it's just something you don't really expect, especially when you're a backup not playing as much."

Kavanagh took a knee on the game's final play with 30 seconds left and it was over. The Badgers had accomplished their goals: they were Big Ten champions and would be heading to the Rose Bowl for a second straight season. Dayne had the record and in a few weeks would add the Heisman Trophy. It was time to celebrate.

With the capacity crowd belting out a heartfelt version of "Varsity," ABC's Leslie Gudel corralled Dayne on the field for the customary post-game interview. The two were soon engulfed by a huge throng of media trying to get Dayne's first reactions to the historic day. Gudel, in her second year with ABC Sports, asked

Dayne more than a half-dozen questions and he answered each with his usual unemotional, brief and to-the-point style. He was, as always, polite and smiling. He simply was not wordy. It was the same public demeanor he had presented through his entire career. Gudel had, of course, met Dayne in the days prior to the game, but was not as familiar with him as the Madison media were. In fact, she has always believed her post-game chat with Dayne did not go as well as it could have, despite the magnitude of the moment.

"There was a picture of me interviewing Ron afterward and all the people around us," Gudel recalled. "I've since gotten that picture. I had it blown up and framed and it's hanging with some of the other sports things I have in my basement. It's special to me. It was such a telling moment about how important it was. It was me and Ron and all these people and flashes going off and cameras rolling. It was this moment I was trying to have with Ron and it was shared with all these people and I remember Ron not saying a whole lot. I was trying everything I could not to ask him a 'yes or no' question. You want him to embellish on the moment. That was one of the toughest interviews I've ever done because to me it was such a meaningful interview and Ron didn't have a lot to say. I know that's how he interviewed, but I remember so much wanting him to break out a little bit and not getting that from him and knowing, when he walked away, that I know he loved the moment, but gosh it would be great to hear him say that. It was just a very difficult thing not to get a little more out of him."

UW athletic department officials had been planning the postgame festivities for days. Among the things discussed was a way to recognize and honor Dayne's career and, hopefully, his breaking of Williams' record. The decision was made to place Dayne's number and last name on the façade of the stadium. Jim's Sign Shop in Waunakee, Wisconsin, created the signage and the covering that went over it (they also created a replacement number 33 in 2000 when the original was stolen from the stadium). Unbeknownst to the team, it was affixed to the façade after football practice in the middle of the week, before the game. Malchow wondered if anyone would notice.

"I remember asking John Chadima if he thought anyone would see it," Malchow said. "When we ended up getting the covering on it, it was pretty neat – you had to know it was there."

Earlier in the week athletic department personnel did a practice run to prepare for the setting up of the postgame on the field. They rolled stages out, determined placement, and tried to map out exactly how things would develop, who would be speaking and what the order of events would be. Eventually a postgame script was finalized. But it was as that script was being executed after the game that something completely unscripted happened.

McArthur Towel of Baraboo, Wisconsin, has been making towels since 1865 and, in more recent years, had created products like the "Terrible Towel" made famous at Pittsburgh Steelers' home games. As Dayne neared the rushing record, McArthur approached American Family Insurance about sponsoring a commemorative towel that could be distributed at the Wisconsin-Iowa game. American Family came aboard and the two companies brought the idea to UW athletic department officials, who enthusiastically embraced the concept. Mike Unitan, then the director of marketing in the athletic department, gathered his staff and they came up with the look of the towels. McArthur did not get approval of the artwork on the towels until around 5 p.m. on the day before the Badgers' November 6 game at Purdue.

McArthur began printing more than 65,000 towels on the following Monday, completed the work by Thursday and delivered the towels to Camp Randall Stadium in time for them to be distributed to fans as they entered the stadium. Meanwhile, an e-mail had gone out to American Family employees asking for volunteers to hand out the towels outside the stadium before the game. The response was overwhelming.

Throughout the game, Badger fans waved and twirled the towels, particularly in the moments after Dayne's record-breaking run. It was, however, during the playing of a tape of Queen's "We Are the Champions," (combined with some Badger football radio highlights) as the stage was being prepared on the field for speakers and presenters, that one of the most spine-tingling moments in UW athletics history took place.

Believed to have started in the student section, fans began to display the towels by holding them up out in front of their faces. Soon the entire stadium was a mass of white towels and red 33's. It was literally a "white out." There had been no instruction to do so on the scoreboard or from Mahnke on the P.A. It was a totally spontaneous show of emotion and appreciation and community, and it remains as memorable to those who were there as anything else that happened that day.

"The most powerful thing for me, it just seemed to get quiet and everybody held up their Ron Dayne towels," Behnke said. "It was literally the entire stadium, holding up the towels in solidarity, and it was really cool the see the number 33 in every section."

Behnke wasn't alone in his assessment. Players, coaches and fans, alike were awed by the moment.

Guard Dave Costa: "I remember the towels – the white towels. I think I still have three of them."

Wayne Esser, Mendota Gridiron Club: "It's in my basement right underneath a picture of Elroy (Hirsch) and Pat Richter. Everybody held them up like they were practicing it. It was like the old card sections. When you see it, that really makes you remember that day."

Guard Bill Ferrario: "I actually have one hanging in my basement. Looking up, you couldn't see a face in the crowd. All you could see was pure white, everybody holding up the towels. Of all the things we accomplished as a team, I think that was the most powerful image, seeing 70 or 80,000 people all holding up the same towel at the same time for the same reason."

Butch Gebhardt, Badger fan: "My best friend, who I was with that day and who I've been to all the Badger games with, has the towel framed with the ticket and I have the next day's newspaper framed with the ticket. I have about three of the towels."

Judy Lowell, American Family Insurance: "Nobody made an announcement about holding up the towels, people just did it spontaneously and I must admit I was a little overwhelmed – it was so cool!"

Rick Nelson, 1999 UW football senior manager: "That made me want to cry. No one will ever experience anything like that again."

Jim Hueber, Badger offensive line coach: "I just remember that stadium at the end. I think somewhere along the line we knew he was going to [break the record]. It was just how the stadium reacted and the towels that they had. And I don't know that we knew about the towels before we went out there as a team. So, when it happened, I think it kind of took us all aback for a second."

Mike Unitan, UW athletics marketing director in 1999: "To me that is still the most magical moment ever at Camp Randall. Breaking the record was incredible and all the celebrations we had, but having the fans, almost on cue, hold up those towels … it's still, to this day, the most amazing thing I've seen our fans do. It was like it was part of the program. I've never seen anything like that that wasn't coordinated beforehand."

Skip McGregor, Badger fan: "I sort of get the chills thinking about it. It was such a magical day. I have a towel framed with a ticket. It hangs in my basement."

Running back Ron Dayne: "It was crazy, just crazy. Amazing."

The visually stunning and heartwarming scene with the towels was there for a few moments and then it was gone. It was time for more magic.

Malchow grabbed Dayne and tried to prepare him for what was coming next.

"I remember walking up to him with people all around us and I put my hand on his shoulder pad and I just said, 'Congratulations on an extremely special season and something amazingly cool is about to happen and you're going to have to address the crowd.' And he said, 'What's that?' I said, 'Your name is on the façade,' and I pointed over my shoulder. 'It's covered up there and they're going to unveil that – it's going to be an unbelievable moment for you and you're going to have to address the crowd.' I said, 'It's not a long speech, you just need to tell them 'thank you for supporting me my whole career, it's great to be a Badger,' or something along those lines.' And he just looked at me bewildered but said, 'That's cool.' And when it got to that point, he delivered in typical Ron fashion."

Alvarez, Richter and Badger captains Dayne, McIntosh, Doering, Ghidorzi and Thompson joined emcee Jeff Tyler on the stage as Robert Vowels, associate commissioner of the Big Ten Conference, presented the players with the conference championship trophy.

"I think it was probably the biggest event I've been a part of in college athletics," said Vowels, who is now with the NCAA. "Watching that record being broken, I can't remember ever being a part of anything else like that."

Vowels handed the trophy to Thompson and McIntosh and the two, smiling proudly, held it up for the fans – now screaming and madly twirling the Dayne towels – to see.

Ken and Barbara Burrows of the Tournament of Roses Committee then made the official invitation to Richter, Alvarez and the team to represent the Big Ten in the 2000 Rose Bowl game on New Year's Day. Alvarez replied to Burrows: "We accept that invitation with pride, and we'll represent the Big Ten with pride."

Alvarez spoke further to the crowd and introduced Dayne, before Richter took the mic.

"It's rare in our lifetime that we get a chance to be in the midst of greatness," Richter told the crowd. "Today and the last four years we have been well honored to be in the presence of Mr. Ron Dayne." Richter then put his hand on Dayne's left shoulder and said, "Ron, in recognition of your great accomplishments, the University of Wisconsin wants to have you take a look up here on the façade at how you will be remembered forever by the Badger fans of the University of Wisconsin." Richter pointed Dayne in the direction of the stadium façade on the upper deck.

One of the UW athletic facilities and maintenance staff members who helped pull the covering back from Dayne's name and number was Chuck Bruhn. He had gone up to where the covering was with about five minutes left in the fourth quarter. What he found when he got there were frustrated fans.

"The covering was tied onto the railing and [the ropes] were blocking some of their view of the game," Bruhn said. "We were trying to tell them it was a special event, but whoever was in charge must not have told them about it. We were sitting right down in front of [those fans] and taking a lot of heat at the time. They were cool with it once they found out what it was. But for a time, they probably wanted to throw us over the upper deck."

Once Richter was finished, Chadima cued Bruhn and his partner to remove the covering.

"It was shocking because we were practicing in there for two days and never saw it," Dayne said of the gray covering over his name and number. "We'd switch sides, go back and forth on both sides, run up and down and never see it. Nobody noticed it. We didn't see it during the game, nothing. That was real shocking for me – it was a big surprise."

Dayne may have been shocked, but a huge smile creased his face. He was given the microphone so he could address the fans and, in what Malchow called "Ron fashion," spoke very briefly: "I just want to say thank you to all you fans. I love you all."

Most who knew Dayne's reputation for being rather humble and quiet were not at all surprised by his brief statement. But Dayne says he kept his comments short because Malchow told him he would be coming back onto the field again. Dayne assumed Malchow meant he would have the opportunity to address the fans one more time. It's likely that Malchow was actually referring to the Senior Day custom of the Badger seniors returning to the field to partake in the UW Band's "Fifth Quarter" celebration. Dayne and Malchow had spent hours and hours together during the running back's career, so it is ironic that this minor miscommunication may have prevented Dayne from saying all he wanted to say to the Badger fans.

The formal post-game ceremony gave way to the Fifth Quarter as Dayne and his teammates headed for the locker room. Obviously it had been a breathtaking afternoon for Wisconsin fans, but it had also touched the visitors from Iowa.

"After the games, I was usually go over to the visiting team side, just to make sure they get off the field and into their locker room," said Alan Fish, then the administrative officer for UW athletics and sport administrator in charge of football. "It was during the celebration and I was talking to two or three Iowa coaches and staff who were standing there watching the whole scene as it was going on. One of them turned to me and said, 'This is really an amazing atmosphere. This is really a classy way to do this.' They said this is something they would like to emulate at Iowa. At that time, they were in a low ebb and so they were looking at us as a role model for what they wanted to become. Well, that hadn't happened at Wisconsin for 30 years. Other Big Ten teams coming here and saying, 'We want to be like you?' To me, one of the goals for the whole athletic department, and especially for football, was to become a leader and model and that was the day we got there, in the eyes of our peers."

Bielema confirmed a similar sentiment.

"The environment that was here (for the '99 game) … it was our first game here at Wisconsin under Kirk Ferentz and things were really rolling here and the game-day environment was second to none," Bielema said. "I distinctly remember our Sunday staff meeting the day after. We went in and sat down, and Kirk always started the meeting with a couple comments. The one thing he said was that if we could ever get the environment they had at Wisconsin yesterday in Iowa City, we've arrived. That made a huge statement to me at the time about how impressive this place was."

Alvarez and Dayne would soon appear together at the post-game news conference on the first floor of the McClain Center. It was there that Dayne told the assembled media that, upon seeing his name unveiled inside the stadium, "I didn't know what to say. I was amazed and dazed. I was happy and grateful. I didn't know whether to laugh or cry." For someone who wasn't always very expressive, Dayne not only summed up his own feelings, but the feelings of many others when they try to describe the special day that was November 13, 1999.

Dannielle Dirienzo was a Badger football fan who grew up just a few blocks from the stadium and attended the game with her mother. She posted her summary of the game, and her experience in the stadium that afternoon, to an old electronic newsgroup the day after the game. It's an interesting look at a precursor to the plethora of blogs and message boards that exist now, 10 years later. Her note read:

Well, here goes...this'll probably be kinda long. :-)

We left to walk up to the game around 2:00 and was struck by how many people were lined up to get in (usually there aren't lines this long a ½ hour before the game). Right inside the gates they were giving out commemorative towels to each fan (large white towels with DAYNE and a 33 on them in Red and with A Tribute to Ron Dayne, Wisconsin vs.

Iowa, November 13, 1999 printed on them). I got up to my seat in time to watch the band march on, but the most exciting pregame thing to watch was the introduction of the seniors. Of course, RD was left till last and to say he received a thunderous ovation when he ran on would be a BIG understatement!

This was THE most electric crowd at a game I've ever been to...whenever Ron had a carry (even if it was only a yard) the entire crowd would yell RON DAYYYYYNNNNNNE (imitating the announcer). There was a DAYNE-METER on top of a building that I could see from my seat, which had a big 99 on it before the game and the numbers were changed as needed throughout.

Throughout the first and second quarters, he was getting so little yardage on his carries, I was kinda wondering if we'd have to wait till the 2nd half to see him break the record. What was even more amazing is that, for awhile, Bollinger had more rushing yards than RD! But when Ron busted that one carry for 30+ yards, you knew it was a matter of time...

The incredible noise and hysteria of the fans when he broke the record just didn't translate to the ABC tapes that well...I could hardly take any pictures since there were so many towels in my face! His teammates came and mobbed him on the sidelines, Pat Richter briefly came onto the field, shook his hand, gave Ron the game ball (he gave it to Bernie Wyatt) and after a few minutes, they started the game again. I can't let this description go without mentioning the streaker that came onto the field (from Section Q) ran down the middle of the field and was eventually arrested in the end zone in front of the Field House. I'm sure THAT picture didn't make it onto ABC...

Of course, RD got more cheers with every carry and, eventually, he had his last carry with not too much time left in the 3rd quarter. He received a standing ovation as he came off the field...

About the only thing of note that happened in the 4th quarter was how the crowd latched onto Matt Unertl. I think they just liked the sound of his name, because since he was getting a lot of carries, every time the announcer said his name, the entire crowd yelled MATT UNERRRRRTL.

If you saw it on TV, that's what they were yelling...

After the game was over, they quickly set up a small stage on the field, where they first had a representative from the NCAA present Barry and Pat with the Big 10 Championship Trophy (Champs outright this time!), then representatives from the Tournament of Roses invited Wisconsin to the Rose Bowl (which Barry accepted). Barry talked for a little bit, and then introduced Ron to the microphone. It was during this time that the most amazing sight I've ever seen in Camp Randall happened.

It began in the student section...they were all standing and holding their 33 towels in front of them...this gradually spread to the entire stadium. It was enough to bring tears to your eyes – you could hardly see anyone in the stands – you saw nothing but almost 80,000 number 33 towels all throughout the stadium. I know this was shown on ABC but to be there in person was incredible...in fact my mother turned to me and *she* was crying!

Pat Richter asked Ron to look at the facade of the upper deck to see how he would be remembered by Wisconsin fans...on the upper deck facade, in big red numbers and letters, they unveiled a permanent 33 – DAYNE next to the CAMP RANDALL STADIUM. This brought thunderous cheers and a big smile to Ron's face (he said later he didn't know whether to laugh or cry when he saw it). Ron said a few words, mainly "Thank you. I love you guys". Sporadically through this ceremony, "We Are The Champions" was blaring from the loudspeaker and they replayed season highlights (off the radio) plus Matt LePay's call of Ron's record setting run.

Eventually the team left the field and the fifth quarter got started. During the 5th quarter, a large percentage of the team came out to celebrate (Ron said later he wanted to, but he knew he'd get mobbed, so he didn't).

I think the best thing came when I was leaving the stadium. We leave on the upper deck side, so while we were walking, we noticed lots of people were looking up at the side of the stadium looming above.

It was pitch black outside, but coming from somewhere, thanks to a large light and a big stencil, there was a HUGE number 33 being shown on the side of the upper deck. The numbers had to be 10-15 feet high...It just took my breath away to look at it...I've never heard this mentioned or seen a photo, so remember you heard it here first...

There were other little touches during the game...Bucky briefly dressed in gold and was striking Heisman poses all over the place...the guy in the section next to us who had the stuffed beaver with a little fake jersey on with "Jerry" on it...the other guy who was walking around with a white helmet on which had a piece of wood attached to the top and on top of that was a small replica of the Heisman trophy.

The Capital Times had printed up an Extra version of Saturday's paper which had just gotten delivered to a nearby street corner as we were leaving. It was a huge (2-3 inch) headline that said "DAYNE IS NO. 1" with a big color picture of Ron...they must've printed these things *so* quick that afternoon! The State Journal the next day had the headline "HISTORIC DAYNE" as a headline...

To say this was the biggest day in Wisconsin sports history is an understatement...I'm just so glad to have gotten the chance to go.

dannielle
hope that wasn't too wordy :-)

Dirienzo was not the only one who felt the way she did.

Andy Baggot, *Wisconsin State Journal*: "A hundred years from now people are going to look back on Wisconsin athletics and they're going to look for the perfect day and that might have been one of those days that you're going to say 'think about all the good things that happened that day.' Ron Dayne certainly solidifies himself as a Heisman Trophy winner and sets the NCAA record, you clinch a berth in the Rose Bowl for the second straight year. All the dominoes fell into place. It was too good to be true. You couldn't sit there at the start of the day and think 'this is going to happen, this is going to happen, this is going to happen.' It would have sounded like a fairy tale. But when all those things fell into place, it was remarkable. It was a magical aspect to that season."

Head coach Barry Alvarez: "I don't know how it could be better. The year before we clinched against Penn State, but it wasn't like that. I don't know if I've ever been in a better atmosphere – with everything falling into place."

Matt Lepay, the radio voice of the Badgers: "Look at this happening at Wisconsin. This doesn't happen here. This happens at Ohio State, Michigan, USC, Texas. They're going to the Rose Bowl again? They're going to have the Heisman Trophy winner who just broke Ricky Williams' record? It was fun for me to see the joy. Fans here went through a long period where they suffered. And now they're seeing a Heisman Trophy winner. They're seeing a team win the Big Ten title again, go to the Rose Bowl again. It was different because the first time they clinched it was in Tokyo, the year before (1998) was cool, but this one had everything. They're beating the daylights out of a rival that for years the story had been reversed. Dayne's breaking the record. He's going to win the Heisman, they're going to the Rose Bowl. And the fans were eating it up. It was fun to watch."

Alia Dayne, Ron's wife: "The energy of the people of Wisconsin was unbelievable. I don't think I felt like that other than at the Super Bowl when Ray Charles sang 'America the Beautiful.' That's as close as I've gotten to getting those tingles."

Fullback Chad Kuhns: "It just gave me chills when they took off that sheet and showed the Dayne 33, and everybody in the whole stadium had their Dayne 33 towels – it was just a magical feeling – I can't explain it, it just gave me chills. We were playing for Ron and what he was able to accomplish and what we were able to help him accomplish as a team."

Ron Dayne left Camp Randall Stadium that night and visited with his family before heading home to his apartment near the Kohl Center carrying a big bottle of champagne that girlfriend, Alia, had given him. Dayne later went out and walked all over Madison, his champagne in tow, celebrating with friends and enjoying himself. If anyone had earned it, he did.

Ten years after it happened, Dayne feels like he has run into countless numbers of people who not only have told him they were at the game, but how much he meant to them.

"I probably met more people than we had at the game that said they were at the game," Dayne said. "It's just 'Oh man, I was there, my family was there. My dad was there, my uncle and grandpop.' I met a couple people that said I kind of brought their family together because they would sit down and have family day and watch me play. People have said, 'You got me and my dad back together, hanging out, we're buddies now and we're tight just because we used to sit down and watch you every Saturday. No matter what, we watched you. And I was even at the game when you broke the record.' I always hear that, no matter what."

The "Dayne Game" was, indeed, meaningful to individual Badger fans, but also to the community as a whole.

"I remember it being a very, very big deal, especially in the minority community," said Barry Fox, the UW athletic department's director of facilities at the time. "I remember going to the barber shop on the south side to get my hair cut and everyone was saying, 'Ron Dayne's gonna do it, Ron Dayne's gonna do it.' It was a big deal. It got brought into the churches, too. I remember our pastor said, 'Say a prayer for Ron.'"

Fish saw the meaning in the way Wisconsinites embraced Dayne and the Badgers of the 1990s, as well.

"During the '90s, we became not just the community's team,

we became the state's team," Fish said. "With the great run that the Packers had in that period of time, it was a place where sports were celebrated at a high level. But I think it's more than that. It also has meaning for the university as a whole, and our connections with the community and state. When I got hired by Donna Shalala in 1989, one of her theories was that the rest of the state still was suspicious and resentful of the Madison campus because of the protests and the bombings, and the Vietnam War protests and the tear gassing. They just felt it was another world, one they didn't relate to. And her theory was, if we can become good in sports, especially football, that will be our campus' entrée back into the rest of the state. We saw that beginning to happen when Pat Richter was first hired and we went all around the state. We would go into communities and there would not be anything that said Wisconsin, or anything red anywhere, once we left the city of Madison. We did a similar tour after the '99 season and whether you were in Superior, Ashland, Antigo, Manitowoc, Bayfield, LaCrosse, people would show up wearing Wisconsin Rose Bowl hats, Wisconsin jackets, sweaters, T-shirts. It was the embodiment of exactly what Donna was looking for – we'd become the state's team. And she wanted to use that as a way to build another bridge back to the state for this campus. And that was a completely unreserved success."

The 1999 Wisconsin football season was just one part, albeit a big one, of a greater step forward for Badger athletics in 1999-2000. In addition to the remarkable achievements of Dayne and the football team, the Wisconsin men's basketball team shocked the college basketball world by playing its way into the Final Four in Indianapolis. The women's basketball team won the WNIT. The men's and women's cross country programs won Big Ten titles. Led by freshman Dany Heatley, the men's hockey team was ranked No. 1 in the nation during the regular season and won the WCHA regular-season crown. The men's track and field program won conference indoor and outdoor titles. An entire athletic department, spearheaded by the football program's quantum leap, was moving to another level.

"To me, we had set a new bar for ourselves, for the entire program," said Fish. "Permanently. As permanently as you can be in college sports. If we're going to go to the Rose Bowl three years out of six and, in the end, actually win three Rose Bowls, and having been to bowl games now multiple years in a row, without any drop, now we were at a different place. Now we were thinking every year, let's play Michigan, let's play Ohio State, instead of having that be something you worried or feared. Now that was a highlight. While the '93 Rose Bowl was the breakout, the '99 season was the year we said, 'We're in a different place entirely, and we need to sustain this level.'"

One area in particular that benefitted almost directly from Dayne and the success of the Badgers of the late 1990s was Camp Randall Stadium itself. Certainly the breakout 1993 season showed that Wisconsin was capable of success on the football field. But Dayne's arrival, the interest that his presence helped create for the program and, subsequently, the huge games the Badgers were involved in – the 1999 Iowa game among them – played a major role in helping to push forward the renovation of the stadium in the early years of this century. Fox remembers exactly where he was when Dayne made his 31-yard run to break Williams' record.

"I got a call to go to the west side [of the stadium] because they were having problems," Fox said. "I'll never forget when Ron broke the record. I was on the west side ankle deep in raw sewage because the toilets had all backed up."

Fish felt that the "Dayne Game" solidified a potential stadium renovation.

"Actually, I turned to some people on the sideline when [Ron] set the record and said, 'We just got our new stadium,' Fish recalled. "Opportunities like that come with a combination of preparation and the alignment of what events are supporting. We had an old stadium for a long time, but we had been filling it up for six or seven years straight and we were having a lot of infrastructure problems.

"This was the year after we opened the Kohl Center, so we had spent a tremendous amount of energy – both resources, time and communication plans – to get the Kohl Center done, and we had said our next job is to renovate Camp Randall Stadium. During the Kohl Center design, we brought architects over here and started thinking about how we could do this on this site. In fact, we had drawn up this plan on the back of a napkin years before we actually designed it because it was the only place we could expand. We could fill in the Field House and we could build suites and club seats over the road between the Shell and East Campus and there wasn't much else we could do."

The program had reached heights never before seen in Madison and the momentum that had been created eventually led to the stadium renovation completed in 2005.

The Badgers went on to knock off Stanford, 17-9, in the Rose Bowl on New Year's Day of 2000. Dayne, of course, led the way with 200 yards and a touchdown on 34 carries. He had finished the season with 2,034 yards (bowl included) and 20 touchdowns and was the nation's second-leading rusher with a 166.7-yard average, despite sitting out six full quarters in blowout wins. His 2,034 yards, in fact, were more than all but four Big Ten teams in 1999. He had won his third Big Ten rushing crown and had been at his best when the Badgers needed it most. He was the consensus player of the year in college football in 1999 and, of course, won the Heisman Trophy.

Ron Dayne's impact on the UW athletic program can be measured in many ways, the renovated stadium being one of them. Summing up Dayne as a runner is somewhat more challenging because there are so many intangibles. Bollinger saw patience.

"The understated thing about Ron was his patience," Bollinger said. "He was as good as I've ever been around at understanding how to be patient in the backfield and how to wait for his blocks, hit his landmarks in the zone running game over and over again, and be patient hitting those landmarks until somebody over-pursues and he hits a crease. I think that's what separated him because I think there are a lot of talented guys. He had a lot of other things going for him, but I think that's what made him what he was as a runner."

Alvarez knew that Dayne wasn't just a straight-ahead, "smash-mouth" runner.

"He was not a bulldozer," Alvarez said. "When he got lathered up and he got worked up, that's how he ran, but Ron was more of a patient runner, more of a deliberate runner. He had good enough vision, he could plant that back foot and make that back-door cut. We adjusted our zone play and our stretch play for him. Terrell Fletcher was so fast he'd just take off running and we'd get him on the edge. Ronnie wasn't that fast, so we adjusted everything to where he'd aim to the inside, to the tight end. He made his read there and made the cut or the inside zone, he had good enough vision to see a seam. But he was a patient runner, not as you would visualize a 255-pounder sticking his head in there moving the pile."

Dayne, of course, could run opponents over just like he could make them miss. Former teammate Nick Davis remembers Dayne's pure power.

"Just a runaway freight train," Davis said of Dayne. "I remember my freshman year the first time I saw him, we put the pads on and we were doing goal line and he just lowered his shoulder and a freshman defensive back just went flying off of him. He had the ability to generate so much power and be able to use that power within the running style. There are a lot of good, strong running backs, but they don't know how to use it. Ron knew how to use it and when to use it. Ron wasn't only a good runner, he was important in the passing game, too, because he would use his power to block. He made a conscious effort in blocking and took pride in it as well. When I think of Ron, I think of a complete player."

Several years after Dayne's playing career had ended at Wisconsin, ESPN presented a list of its 25 greatest college football players. Dayne was not on the list, most likely because he wasn't flashy and, in the minds of some, didn't play for a "traditional" power. It could not have been because of a lack of production on the field, a lack of importance to the school at which he played or a lack of appreciation from the fans who cheered him on. If those were the criteria by which great college football players were judged, Ron Dayne's name would appear in the same spot it appears on the NCAA rushing list. At the top.

"What he did, the home he came from, the drugs that were involved in his family, his situation was not the greatest," said Baggot. "He's really one of the greater success stories that I've ever come across in high school, college or professional athletics. And to have done it without really changing how he lived his life. He was a pretty humble guy coming in and he left as a pretty humble guy. The fact that he settled here, he's going to be beloved as long as he's around here. I think especially the further you get away from it – 10 years – people get a greater appreciation for that achievement because it's awesome. The Heisman? There are people who pan that award now, but that's an honor. You really have to be something special to win the Heisman."

That's exactly what Ron Dayne was.

CHAPTER NINE
The Heisman

Ron Dayne's uncle, Rob Reid, was talking to a reporter from the *Philadelphia Inquirer* during the summer of 1997 when he said, "Look at this." Reid showed the writer a watch from the 1996 Copper Bowl, the first bowl game his nephew had played in, before he continued. "Ron came home from that game and said, 'Here, I've got something for you for being so great to me.' You know," Reid said to the reporter, "if he won the Heisman Trophy, Ron would probably bring it here and say, 'this is yours.'"

Reid had no idea how prophetic that statement would turn out to be.

Ron Dayne's performance on November 6 at Purdue pushed him to the front of the Heisman Trophy pack. The major media outlets, including *USA Today*, CNN/*SI*, *The Sporting News* and Fox Sports, along with the Scripps Howard poll, all had him atop their Heisman polls heading into the regular-season finale against Iowa. Georgia Tech quarterback Joe Hamilton would put together an astounding performance – 322 passing yards, 88 rushing yards and five touchdown passes in a 45-42 win over Clemson – on the same day that Dayne broke Ricky Williams' record with his 216-yard, one-touchdown outing (in three quarters) against the Hawkeyes. But the momentum that the Badgers, and Dayne, had created since the loss to Michigan proved to be too much for anyone else to overcome.

Dayne spent much of the early part of December on the college football awards circuit with sports information director Steve Malchow. He had been working with Malchow and Doug Tiedt, his academic advisor, on a speech he could give if he were to win the Heisman.

"Ron would never tell you that he hoped he would win it," Tiedt said. "But he was excited about it. I spoke with him, I think it was in the locker room after he broke the record, and I think I told Malchow I was going to start working on the Heisman speech with Ron. Ron and I had talked a bit about it and he wasn't sure he'd even know what to say. So when we started working on it, we'd go through all the stuff that he might want to say."

Malchow had been worrying because Dayne hadn't shown or read him a speech, and the trips to Orlando for the college football awards show and, eventually, New York City for the Heisman presentation were quickly approaching.

"One night I was just laying at home in bed and kind of thinking about it," Malchow said. "What came to me was, this is really simple. What Ron ought to do is just get up there and say 'I want to thank everybody with the Heisman Trophy' and then think of the five or six or eight people that have meant a lot to you. All we're going to do is memorize those people's names and then you're going to say one thing about each person. And that's the speech. So, I'm lying there in bed and I almost kind of recite something out loud for his speech."

The next day, in his office, Malchow recounted for Dayne the essence of the speech he had conjured up the night before. Dayne then began to formulate some of his thoughts.

"I started writing it down, just to kind of get used to doing it," Dayne said. "I had some ideas from Steve – make it like five parts. Then I went to Doug Tiedt and he helped me. He kind of helped me write up something, then I just kind of put it in my own words and rehearsed it."

Tiedt helped Dayne by putting together a small booklet of

index cards, with red plastic binding, that contained an outline Dayne could refer to as he practiced his speech.

"It just became a list of thank you's," Tiedt said. "That's all he could get to is thanking all these people that had been important in his life. So, he wrote it and we typed it up and talked about him memorizing it and he said he would try and we put it on some little cards. I think we did two or three of them that we'd keep in different spots for him to look at. It wasn't that he couldn't remember stuff; he just didn't want to forget anyone's name. He had all these people in his life and he didn't want to forget anybody."

Malchow and Dayne took off for Orlando, with Malchow becoming increasingly concerned because the running back still had not shared his speech with him. The two landed in Florida late at night, hoping to avoid the crowds of autograph-seeker who were following Dayne everywhere. Dayne just wanted to get to his hotel room and relax. It had been a long year and this was going to be a lengthy trip. But they were followed anyway.

"What had happened was, when we were in Detroit, somebody spotted him and called to the autograph seekers in Orlando and told them what flight we were on," Malchow recalled. "So, here we thought we had avoided all of that and we had been scouted out in Detroit. So we sat there for maybe a half hour and signed. We had to get checked into the hotel and get ready for tomorrow's activities. But it shows the notoriety he had."

Malchow and Dayne made it to the hotel in Orlando and checked in.

"I got to my room and my phone rang and it was Ron," Malchow said. "And he asks me what I'm doing. I told him I was getting unpacked and he asks me if I want to hear his speech. And I said, 'You have a speech?' So I went down to his room and he says, 'Do you want me to use paper or should I just do it off the top of my head?' I told him I'd prefer he do it off the top of his head. So, he delivered the speech and I just got tears in my eyes – it was awesome. It was so genuine, it was totally Ron, it was Ron's language, it was totally from the heart, and I just went up and shook his hand and told him I'd been worried for a long time, but that he just hit a home run. What he ended up delivering on TV, he threw in a few extras, did a little freelancing there, but by and large it was fairly solid. It wasn't as good as the solo perform-ance that I saw in his hotel room in Orlando, but it was certainly acceptable. He thanked people as I think he was happy to do and it went great."

Dayne earned the Maxwell and Doak Walker Awards as well as the Walter Camp Player of the Year Award at the Home Depot College Football Awards Show in Lake Buena Vista, Florida. His speech was ready and he had won just about every individual award he could. All that was left was the trip to New York.

The Heisman experience was, needless to say, a memorable and emotional experience for all who had in some way been involved with the four-year odyssey that had brought Dayne to the Downtown Athletic Club.

"I remember getting there at the airport and they had a limo to pick us up," Malchow said. "And Ron and I shared a limousine ride with Chad Pennington, and I remember just being extremely impressed with how bright he was and how excited he was. I remember Michael Vick being there. Just like Ron, he had the mil-lion-dollar smile. The rooms we stayed in at the Downtown Athletic Club were extremely dated, very tiny. My hotel phone did-n't work. And cell phones weren't prevalent then the way they are now. So, I got hardly any phone calls because no one could reach me."

Had Malchow's phone worked, he might have received a call from Dayne's mother, Brenda. She rode to New York in a car with her ex-husband and an aunt and uncle of Ron's. The car had passed the hotel when it slid into a guard rail. No one was hurt, but Brenda got out of the car, grabbed her suitcase and ran the rest of the way to the hotel, where her son had told her to meet him on the seventh floor. She finally got there and went to Ron's room with him. He asked her what had happened and she replied, "You don't want to know."

Malchow remembers being awed by the facility during a pre-ceremony walk-through.

"When you walked into the actual room and you saw the oil paintings (of the previous Heisman winners), I just got goose-bumps," Malchow said. "It was unbelievable because we got a chance to do a walk-through and get the lay of the land. I didn't really have any idea if he'd won – I liked Ron's chances but I didn't know. Then the day of, it was kind of interesting. Some ESPN folks came up and they started asking me questions about who was going to be there. Where would Alia and Jada be sitting? Are Ron's parents going to be there? Where are Rob and Debbie Reid sitting? And I started thinking, 'Holy cow, they're asking where people are sitting, he must have won.' Well then, all of a sudden I saw them doing that with one of the other sports information directors and I thought, 'Okay, they must be doing that with everybody.' I was just trying to get a tip if he had won."

Baggot traveled to New York to cover the event with fellow *Wisconsin State Journal* reporter Tom Mulhern and photographer Craig Schreiner. Ten years later, Baggot still has extraordinarily fond memories.

"I still have one of those Do Not Disturb signs from the hotel where we stayed," Baggot said. "It's from the World Trade Center Marriott, which went down (in the terrorist attacks on Sept. 11, 2001), so every time I see that, I think of that. We were within walking distance of the Downtown Athletic Club. The Downtown Athletic Club, for a place of such mythic reputation, was, politely, a dump. It really was. But it was a charming dump. I remember looking at Tom Mulhern and saying, 'I can't believe we're really here.' This is a place that is mythical for all of college football. All the great people that have come through there and all the people that were awarded that trophy there, it was such a rare opportunity. I think we appreciated it. I remember Ron had gone to get some awards and he got in the same day we did. He was tired. I remember he had brought a stuffed animal for his daughter. That was something cool about Ron. You didn't just see a student-athlete. You also saw a father. You also saw a guy who had a family. And the more you went through his life, the more you got to see that and I thought that was a pretty neat aspect of it."

Dayne's girlfriend, Alia, was pregnant with the couple's second child and was, of course, also handling two-year-old Jada.

"I just remember freaking out about the seating and they didn't realize how young Jada was and they were going to put us directly behind on national television – with a 2-year-old? Yeah, I don't think so. So it was nice we were off to the side."

Ron Dayne was joined that night inside the cozy Downtown Athletic Club by Marshall's Chad Pennington, Virginia Tech freshman Michael Vick, Purdue's Drew Brees and Georgia Tech's Joe Hamilton. Each player's head coach sat in the row right behind him.

Alvarez had taken the Badgers to the Downtown Athletic Club before their game against Syracuse in the Meadowlands in 1997. Now he was back, and getting a pretty good idea about what was going to happen.

"I was sitting next to (Marshall coach) Bob Pruett who had Pennington there," Alvarez said. "I'm sitting there, they break for the commercial and some girls come running up to Ron and start wiping him off – he was sweating – and putting makeup on him, and they didn't bother the other guys. And Pruett says to me, 'I guess that's a dead giveaway.'"

Moments later ESPN's Chris Fowler introduced Bill Dockery, the president of the Downtown Athletic Club. Dockery welcomed and thanked everyone, talked about the Heisman Trophy and complimented the five finalists. He then uttered the words the Badgers and their fans had been waiting to hear since Dayne had announced he would be coming back to Madison for his senior year: "The Downtown Athletic Club is proud to award the 1999 Heisman Memorial Trophy to ... Ron Dayne of the University of Wisconsin."

Dayne smiled, stood up, shook Pennington's hand and turned to Alvarez. The coach and his talented tailback embraced.

Back in Madison, the Badgers had gathered in the Camp Randall Stadium press box to watch the ceremony. A big-screen television hung on the south wall of the eighth level of the facility. Brian White, Dayne's position coach, and his wife, Salli, were there. So were wide receivers coach Henry Mason and his wife, Debbie. Tauscher, Rabach and Ferrario sat side-by-side in the back row. Everyone erupted when Dayne was announced as the winner.

"I just felt pride because I had personally put so much time and effort into Wisconsin football and this whole thing," guard Dave Costa said. "Ron getting the Heisman was just kind of a validation of all the hard work, especially for an offensive lineman. I think he would've done great in any system. I think he would've come close to the rushing record with a lot of O-lines that were in college football at the time, but to have him get the record and then get the Heisman, I was just proud to be part of it, really. I was proud of Ron, too, because out of anybody, Ron had the most pressure on him. From day one, there was all this hype, a lot of pressure to perform and succeed and do everything the right way and all that stuff. And he did it. In the end, he pulled it off. I was proud for the offensive line, for everybody."

White felt the same sense of pride.

"The press box, that was a magical night," White said. "I'll never forget being up there with my wife, just the sense of anticipation and the way the press box was set up on the recruiting weekend. It was just awesome. It was just really incredible and then to listen to Ron's speech – and I know I'm biased – but it was as in-depth a Heisman speech as I can remember. It was heartfelt, all the people he thanked, he really made it personal. The growth he'd made in his career not just as a football player, but as a person. It was a great moment for me personally, outside of the fact that he won the Heisman Trophy. Just to see and listen to him present such a great speech."

Dayne headed up to the podium to give the acceptance speech that had been of so much concern to Malchow, Tiedt and Alia. It read as follows:

"First I want to give an honor to God for blessing me with my talents. I'd like to thank the Downtown Athletic Club for honoring me with this great award. I want to congratulate the finalists on a great season, even becoming a finalist. I definitely want to congratulate my teammates and my coaches, because if it wasn't for my teammates I wouldn't be here today. I'd like to thank Coach Alvarez for always being there for me. No matter what goes on, Coach Alvarez is there for me, treating me like a son. Coach Wyatt for recruiting me and being a person I can come talk to from the East Coast. Coach White for being the best running backs coach in the country.

"Coach, I don't know what to say. I'm just so honored and blessed that I had you as a coach. You taught me to be a great father. Steve Malchow for helping me with all my media hoopla. Wisconsin's academic staff for just being there for us all the time, every athlete. Doug ... I don't know what to say, there's so many people I'd love to thank. I'd like to thank Hop for being there and believing in me. My mom, my dad, 'Mor-Mor' for being there and supporting me through all my ups and downs. My daughter, Jada, for being the biggest inspiration in my life. My girl, Alia, for being there. My sister for being there for me. Everybody ... Yaz, Willie,

Eddie. Finally, I'd like to thank the real Heisman winner, to me, my Uncle Rob, for always being there for me, having somebody to come talk to, to call on the phone, make jokes and everything. I love you. Thank you again for this great award and I'm honored."

The concerns anyone had about Dayne's speech were laid to rest.

"He gave a great speech!" said Alia. "Probably the best speech he's ever given, then and since. I was sitting there next to Steve (Malchow) and Steve just broke down. Then [he was] back to 'P.R. Steve.' Talk about the unsung hero: Steve Malchow. Unbelievable what that man did to keep Ron on track and track him down. And, of course, Barry Alvarez being there, again being that first person to hug him. For Ron that was a big deal. It couldn't have been written any better."

Rob Reid, who gave Dayne a hug before he could sit down after the speech, was overcome with emotion.

"When they announced his name at the Heisman, I'm like 'Oh my gosh, you've got to be kidding me,'" Reid said. "I was frozen in my seat and, as he began to give his speech, I'm thinking 'My God, Ronnie hates to speak in front of crowds, what's he gonna say, I hope it's the right thing.' I was really nervous. And when he said 'This Heisman really goes to my Uncle Rob,' I was like ... with his dad and his mom there and coaches and everybody ... I broke down. I just could not believe it. And I think I kind of transposed myself, thinking about aspirations I had about playing professional football, maybe winning the Heisman myself, it was all summed up in what he did. It was like it was me receiving the Heisman. When he dedicated it to me, I was completely broken up. I don't think I realized the impact I had on his life. You never think you do enough or maybe you think you do too much. I felt like I was his hero, to be honest with you. I never really felt that or thought that until that day."

Dayne received the trophy itself two days later at a different ceremony in New York. He had one last surprise for his Uncle Rob.

"Ron got to take the trophy home on that Monday," Reid said. "[The announcement] was on Saturday and they had a banquet Monday night, the night they actually give it out. So, they gave him the trophy that night and he called me over and said, 'Here, this is for you. Would you take this?' So, here I am in a taxi cab with the Heisman Trophy, driving back to my hotel. I'm walking into the hotel and people are looking at me like 'Is he carrying the Heisman Trophy?' It was surreal, it was unbelievable. I was walking through the hotel where we had the banquet and people are like 'Is that the Heisman?' It was kind of mind-blowing, me having it in my hands. I'm hoping I don't get robbed or mugged or something, carrying this in downtown New York in a cab back to the hotel. I had it locked in a safe at a bank. I was too fearful to have it in my house. I gave it back to him. I said, 'Ron, you need to have this in your house.' When he finally got his house built, I said, 'This belongs in your house.'"

In the span of about a month's time, Dayne had given away the ball he carried on the play that broke Williams' record, along with the Heisman Trophy. His generosity toward his teammates, his family and his coaches was genuine, just like his Heisman acceptance speech.

Dayne's friend and former teammate Cecil Martin was late into his rookie season with the Philadelphia Eagles when the 1999 Heisman Trophy was officially presented on that Monday evening in New York. Martin made sure he was there.

"I had become a starter in the middle of my rookie year and I was waiting to go to a meeting and I got a chance to see Ron receive the trophy on TV," Martin said. "The next day we played our game. I had talked to Ron and he had said to come down because there was something Monday night. So I had to go to (Eagles' head coach) Andy Reid – and I was scared to do this because I was a rookie – and ask to leave practice early Monday to go down and see Ron get the Heisman. He let me go and I got a chance to go to the official Heisman Trophy reception on Monday night. I remember walking in and Ron was kind of standing by the edge of the stage with a tuxedo on and all the lights were behind him and he had the Heisman with him and he was already a star. He was my teammate, my brother, but in that moment … I remember taking a moment and saying, 'Wow, he did it.'"

Had Dayne known what Martin was thinking at the time, he likely would have corrected his friend and simply said, "*We* did it."

RON DAYNE
RUSHING STATISTICS

ALL GAMES

Year	Att.	Yds.	Avg.	TD
1996	325	2,109	6.5	21
1997	263	1,457	5.5	15
1998	295	1,525	5.2	15
1999	337	2,034	6.0	20
TOTAL	1,220	7,125	5.8	71

BOWL GAMES

Year	Att.	Yds.	Avg.	TD
1996	30	246	8.2	3
1997	14	36	2.6	0
1998	27	246	9.1	4
1999	34	200	5.9	1
TOTAL	105	728	6.9	8

WITHOUT BOWLS

Year	Att.	Yds.	Avg.	TD
1996	295	1,863	6.3	18
1997	249	1,421	5.7	15
1998	268	1,279	4.8	11
1999	303	1,834	6.1	19
TOTAL	1,115	6,397	5.7	63

RON DAYNE
RECEIVING STATISTICS

ALL GAMES

Year	Rec.	Yds.	Avg.	TD
1996	14	133	9.5	0
1997	10	117	11.7	0
1998	6	45	7.5	0
1999	1	9	9.0	0
TOTAL	**31**	**304**	**9.8**	**0**

1996 GAME-BY-GAME RUSHING STATISTICS

Opp.	Att.	Yds.	Avg.	TD
E. Michigan	8	53	6.6	1
@UNLV	13	90	6.9	1
Stanford	12	75	6.3	0
Penn State	23	129	5.4	2
@Ohio State	21	65	3.1	0
Northwestern	28	139	5.0	1
@Mich. State	15	81	5.4	0
Purdue	30	244	8.1	2
Minnesota	50	297	5.9	3
@Iowa	17	62	3.6	0
@Illinois	41	289	7.0	4
@Hawaii	36	339	9.4	4
Utah	30	246	8.2	3
Total	**325**	**2,109**	**6.5**	**21**

1996 Honors

- Third-team all-American by Associated Press
- Honorable mention all-American by Football News
- First-team freshman all-American and Freshman of the Year by The Sporting News
- Philadelphia Inquirer Freshman of the Year
- First-team all-Big Ten by media and second-team by coaches
- Big Ten co-Freshman of the Year
- Big Ten Offensive Player of the Week vs. Purdue, Minnesota and Illinois
- New Jersey Sportswriters Association College Running Back of the Year
- Copper Bowl Most Valuable Player

1997 GAME-BY-GAME RUSHING STATISTICS

Opp.	Att.	Yds.	Avg.	TD
Syracuse	13	46	3.5	0
Boise State	—Did Not Play—			
@San Jose St.	20	254	12.7	3
San Diego St.	26	145	5.6	4
Indiana	34	202	5.9	2
@N'western	25	93	3.7	2
Illinois	28	207	7.4	2
@ Purdue	26	141	5.4	1
@Minnesota	40	183	4.6	1
Iowa	7	24	3.4	0
Michigan	—Did Not Play—			
@Penn State	30	126	4.2	0
Georgia	14	36	2.6	0
Totals	**263**	**1,457**	**5.5**	**15**

1997 Honors

- First-team all-American by Football News
- Semi-finalist for Football News Offensive Player of the Year
- Second-team all-Big Ten by media and coaches
- AT&T Long-Distance Award for 80-yard run at San Jose State
- ABC Player of the Game vs. Penn State
- Dane County Humane Society "You Made a Difference" Award

1998 GAME-BY-GAME RUSHING STATISTICS

Opp.	Att.	Yds.	Avg.	TD
@San Diego St.	—Did Not Play—			
Ohio	20	111	5.6	3
UNLV	13	108	8.3	0
Northwestern	22	168	7.6	1
@Indiana	28	130	4.6	1
Purdue	33	127	3.8	1
@Illinois	39	190	4.9	3
@Iowa	39	164	4.2	1
Minnesota	35	133	3.8	1
@Michigan	16	53	3.3	0
Penn State	23	95	4.1	0
UCLA	27	246	9.1	4
Totals	**295**	**1,525**	**5.2**	**15**

1998 Honors

- First-team all-American by Walter Camp
- Doak Walker Award finalist
- First-team all-Big Ten by coaches and media
- Big Ten Offensive Player of the Week vs. Northwestern and Illinois
- Rose Bowl Most Valuable Player
- ABC Player of the Game vs. UCLA
- Bowl Championship Series MVP
- Sports Illustrated All-Bowl Team
- Wayne Souza Award co-winner

1999 GAME-BY-GAME RUSHING STATISTICS

Opp.	Att.	Yds.	Avg.	TD
Murray St.	20	135	6.8	3
Ball State	31	158	5.1	1
@Cincinnati	28	231	8.3	1
Michigan	22	88	4.0	1
@Ohio State	32	161	5.0	4
@Minnesota	25	80	3.2	1
Indiana	17	167	9.8	2
Mich. State	34	214	6.3	2
@N'western	35	162	4.6	2
@Purdue	32	222	6.9	1
Iowa	27	216	8.0	1
Stanford	34	200	5.9	1
Totals	**337**	**2,034**	**6.0**	**20**

1999 Honors

- Heisman Trophy winner
- Maxwell Award winner
- Doak Walker Award winner
- Associated Press Player of the Year
- Walter Camp Player of the Year
- Football News Player of the Year
- The Sporting News Player of the Year
- Chicago Tribune Silver Football winner (Big Ten Most Valuable Player)
- CNN/SI.com Player of the Year

- First-team all-American by Associated Press, Walter Camp Foundation, American Football Coaches Association, Football Writers Association, The Sporting News, Football News, CNN/SI.com, CBS Sportsline and collegefootball.com
- Big Ten Offensive Player of the Year by coaches and media
- First-team All-Big Ten by coaches and media
- Wisconsin co-MVP (with all-America tackle Chris McIntosh)
- Rose Bowl Most Valuable Player
- Sports Illustrated All-Bowl Team
- Hula Bowl participant
- Big Ten Offensive Player of the Week vs. Cincinnati, Michigan State, Purdue and Iowa
- USA Today National Player of the Week vs. Iowa
- 31-yard run vs. Iowa (to become college football's career rushing leader) was Compaq Play of the Week and was listed by Monday Night Football's Chris Berman as his No. 3 "Play of the Week" on Nov. 15th
- Had his name and number unveiled on the façade of Camp Randall Stadium after his final home game vs. Iowa on Nov. 13
- Dec. 11 was listed as "Ron Dayne Day" by Wisconsin Governor Tommy Thompson and Milwaukee Mayor John Norquist.
- Nov. 13th was recognized as "Ron Dayne Day" by Madison Mayor Sue Bauman.
- UW team captain

BIBLIOGRAPHY

CHAPTER ONE

1. Seven-point underdogs: *Wisconsin State Journal,*
    November 18, 1995 ....pg. 17
2. But the Badgers: Justin Doherty, *Tales From the
    Wisconsin Badgers* (Champaign, Ill., Sports Publishing,
    LLC, 2005), p. 107........................pg. 17
3. Alvarez thought at the time: Barry Alvarez with
    Mike Lucas, *Don't Flinch – Barry Alvarez: The
    Autobiography* (Champaign, Ill., KCI Sports, LLC,
    2006), p. 163.............................pg. 17
4. "Our kids really don't know": *The Capital Times,*
    November 15, 1995; Twenty-five players on the
    current UW roster: *Wisconsin State Journal,*
    November 18, 1995.........................pg. 18
5. "take our whole program": *Milwaukee Journal
    Sentinel,* November 26, 1995. ....pg. 20

CHAPTER TWO

6. Who had known Dayne's family: *Milwaukee Journal
    Sentinel,* March 11, 2000. ....pg. 21
7. Was instrumental in working: *Wisconsin State Journal,*
    January 28, 1996..........................pg. 21
8. Dayne recorded the third-longest: *Sports Illustrated,*
    September 16, 1996, p. 36. ....pg. 24
9. "I was thinking": *Newark Star-Ledger,* June 6,
    1996......................................pg. 24

10. Dayne even provisionally: 1996 *University of Wisconsin Football Media Guide*, p. 101. . . . . .pg. 24

11. Amazingly, he had only: *The Capital Times*, June 3, 1996. . . . . .pg. 24

12. The *Wisconsin State Journal* finally reported: *Wisconsin State Journal*, November 23, 1995. . . . .pg. 25

13. He asked Dayne if he liked: Alvarez, *Don't Flinch*, p. 164. . . . . .pg. 25

CHAPTER THREE

14. John Dettmann came to Wisconsin: http://www.UWBadgers.com. . . . . .pg. 27

15. Kavanagh was a prep All-American: 1996 *University of Wisconsin Football Media Guide*, p. 103. . . . . .pg. 28

16. "Normally we don't have": *Wisconsin State Journal*, August 11, 1996. . . . . .pg. 28

17. When Donnel was about six: *Sports Illustrated*, October 26, 1998, p. 95. .pg. 30

18. Mike Lucas, the longtime: *The Capital Times*, June 3, 1996. . . . . .pg. 33

19. "It's hard for me to say": *Wisconsin State Journal*, August 11, 1996. . . . . .pg. 33

CHAPTER FOUR

20. Alvarez had acknowledged: *The Capital Times*, August 9, 1996. . . . . .pg. 34

21. Baggot gleaned a few nuggets: *Wisconsin State Journal*, August 19, 1996. . . . . .pg. 37

22. "I have never seen": *Wisconsin State Journal*, August 19, 1996. . . . . .pg. 37

23. Alvarez publicly stated: *Wisconsin State Journal*, September 3, 1996. . . . . .pg. 39

24. A collective murmur: *Wisconsin State Journal,* September 8, 1996. . . . . .pg. 39

25. "the biggest curiosity": *Milwaukee Journal Sentinel,* September 7, 1996. . . . . .pg. 40

26. "Everyone wanted to see him": *Wisconsin State Journal,* September 8, 1996. . . . . .pg. 40

27. "UW leaves lots of room to improve": *Wisconsin State Journal,* September 8, 1996. . . . . .pg. 40

28. But Alvarez also added: Final NCAA official statistics packet, Eastern Michigan vs. Wisconsin, September 7, 1996. . . . . .pg. 40

29. "That made me feel good": *Wisconsin State Journal,* September 8, 1996. . . . . .pg. 41

30. "Hey, that's a big cat": *Milwaukee Journal Sentinel,* September 8, 1996. . . . . .pg. 41

31. Wisconsin won the game: *Wisconsin State Journal,* September, 15, 1996. . . . . .pg. 42

32. "I'm sure we'll get him": *Wisconsin State Journal,* September 24, 1996. . . . . .pg. 45

33. "quickly become the people's choice": ABC telecast, Penn State at Wisconsin, September 28, 1996. . . . . .pg. 45

34. "We were just trying to hang in there": *Philadelphia Inquirer,* September 29, 1996. . . . . .pg. 47

35. "Craig 'Ironhead' Heyward dies at 39": Associated Press, May 28, 2006. . . . . .pg. 47

36. "I said at the press conference": *The Capital Times,* October 1, 1996. . . . . .pg. 48

37. Northwestern's Adrian Autry: *Wisconsin State Journal,* October 20, 1996. . . . . .pg. 49

38. "We were over on the sideline relaxing": *Wisconsin State Journal,* October 20, 1996. . . . . .pg. 49

39. "Why are they even": ESPN telecast, Northwestern at Wisconsin, October 19, 1996. . . . . .pg. 50

40. Moments later Danielson added: ESPN telecast, Northwestern at Wisconsin, October 19, 1996; New York Daily News, January 10, 2009. . . . . .pg. 50

41. "Questionable play-calling brings UW to its knees": *Wisconsin State Journal*, October 20, 1996. . . . . . .pg. 51

42. ESPN's Lee Corso: *The Washington Times*, October 24, 1996. . . . . .pg. 51

43. And Nessler later apologized: Ibid. . . . . .pg. 51

44. Alvarez contended that he: Barry Alvarez with Mike Lucas, *Don't Flinch* (Champaign, Ill., KCI Sports LLC, 2006), p. 167. .pg. 51

45. "the Badgers' hopes": *Wisconsin State Journal*, October 27, 1996. . . . . .pg. 52

46. "just getting lathered up": *Wisconsin State Journal*, November 10, 1996. . . . . .pg. 53

47. "I noticed that": *Wisconsin State Journal*, November 10, 1996. . . . . .pg. 54

48. "Someday I'll be telling": *Wisconsin State Journal*, November 24, 1996. . . . . .pg. 56

49. "The kid is a great athlete": *The Capital Times*, November 26, 1996. . . . . .pg. 57

50. "We were going through our script": Alvarez with Lucas, *Don't Flinch*, p. 168. .pg. 58

51. "I like to break records": *Milwaukee Journal Sentinel*, December 2, 1996. . . . . .pg. 59

52. Hawaii defensive coordinator Don Lindsey: Justin Doherty, *Tales From the Wisconsin Badgers* Champaign, Ill., Sports Publishing LLC, 2005), p. 114. . . . . . .pg. 60

53. *USA Today* ran a story: *USA Today*, December 27, 1996. . . . . .pg. 61

54. "When they say Ron Dayne runs smart": ESPN telecast, Wisconsin vs. Utah, December 27, 1996. . . . . .pg. 61

CHAPTER FIVE

55. "They keep talking about (Dayne)": *The Capital Times*, December 28, 1996. . . . . .pg. 63

56. "I was, of course, thrilled": *Wisconsin State Journal*, July 27, 1997. . . . . .pg. 65

57. Senior-to-be running back Carl McCullough: *Wisconsin State Journal*, January 3, 1997. . . . . . .pg. 66

58. "Every kid who plays football": *The Capital Times*, January 9, 1997. . . . . .pg. 66

59. "I think Mac understands": *Wisconsin State Journal*, April 13, 1997. . . . . .pg. 69

60. Johnson, who had been starting: *Wisconsin State Journal*, April 22, 1997. . . . . .pg. 69

61. Dayne and Manning had met: *The Capital Times*, July 16, 1997. . . . . .pg. 69

62. He made the cover: *Wisconsin State Journal*, June 27, 1997. . . . . .pg. 69

63. "I feel more relaxed": *Wisconsin State Journal*, July 27, 1997. . . . . .pg. 70

64. "one of the leading candidates": 1997 University of Wisconsin Football Media Guide, p. 64. . . . . . . .pg. 70

65. "Carl has earned all": *The Capital Times*, August 8, 1997. . . . . .pg. 70

66. Dayne had sustained: *The Capital Times*, August 25, 1997. . . . . .pg. 71

67. "I said before the game": *Houston Chronicle*, August 25, 1997. . . . . .pg. 72

68. "Dayne is bigger than we saw": *Milwaukee Journal Sentinel*, September 14, 1997. . . . . .pg. 78

69. "We run that play a thousand times": *Wisconsin State Journal*, October 20, 1996. .pg. 79

70. "The toughness he brought": Justin Doherty, *Tales From the Wisconsin Badgers* (Champaign, Ill.: Sports Publishing LLC, 2005), p. 117. . . . . .pg. 79

71. Noting Dayne's statistics at the time: *Sports Illustrated*, October 20, 1997. . . . . .pg. 80

72. "He's a load": *Minneapolis Star Tribune*, October 26, 1997. . . . . .pg. 81

CHAPTER SIX

73. "We haven't put the big hype on him": *The Star Ledger*, August 26, 1998. .pg. 92

74. "one of the kindest athletes": Justin Doherty, *Tales From the Wisconsin Badgers* (Champaign, Ill.: Sports Publishing LLC, 2005), p. 124. . . . . .pg. 93

75. "In the locker room": *Wisconsin State Journal*, October 18, 1998. . . . . .pg. 98

76. "the worst team I can remember": Barry Alvarez with Mike Lucas, *Don't Flinch* (Champaign, Ill.: KCI Sports, LLC, 2006), p. 179. . . . . .pg. 100

77. "Some of my reasons": *Wisconsin State Journal*, December 22, 1998. . . . . .pg. 101

78. "Take away Ron Dayne": *Wisconsin State Journal*, January 2, 1999. . . . . .pg. 106

79. "He can overpower you": *Wisconsin State Journal*, January 2, 1999. . . . . .pg. 106

CHAPTER SEVEN

80. "Ron does pretty well": *The Capital Times*, August 4, 1999. . . . . .pg. 111

81. "Sore ankle and key fumble": *Cleveland Plain Dealer*, September 20, 1999. . . . . .pg. 120

82. "I'll never remember": *New Orleans Times Picayune,*
September 25, 1999. . . . . .pg. 120

83. "seemed to fall out of contention": *Boston Globe,*
September 27, 1999. . . . . .pg. 122

84. "Ron Dayne has just": Wisconsin at Ohio State, ABC
television broadcast, October 2, 1999. . . . . . . .pg. 126

85. "The 5'10", 252-pound senior": *Sports Illustrated,*
October 18, 1999. . . . . .pg. 127

86. "things are looking pretty iffy": *Wisconsin State
Journal,* October 16, 1999. . . . . .pg. 127

87. "the final push has to start": *Wisconsin State Journal,*
October 16, 1999. . . . . .pg. 127

88. "Somewhere down the line": *Wisconsin State Journal,*
October 17, 1999. . . . . .pg. 128

89. "one of the best" and "this one required": *Newark
Star Ledger,* October 29, 1999. . . . . .pg. 131

90. "go right at them": Michigan State at Wisconsin,
ESPN2 telecast, October 23, 1999. . . . . .pg. 132

91. "has the potential": *Chicago Sun-Times,* November
3, 1999. . . . . .pg. 133

92. "Now that's a big-time run": Wisconsin at Purdue,
ABC telecast, November 6, 1999. . . . . .pg. 136

CHAPTER EIGHT

93. *Wisconsin State Journal,* November 9, 1999. . . .pg. 141

94. "One of my secrets": Justin Doherty, *Tales From the
Wisconsin Badgers* (Champaign, Ill., Sports Publishing
LLC, 2005), p. 115. . . . . .pg. 155

95. "No one arm tackles this guy": Iowa at Wisconsin,
ABC telecast, November 13, 1999. . . . . .pg. 158

96. "Open up the history books": Iowa at Wisconsin,
ABC telecast, November 13, 1999. . . . . .pg. 161

97. "Ron Dayne has just run": Iowa at Wisconsin, ABC
telecast, November 13, 1999. . . . . .pg. 175

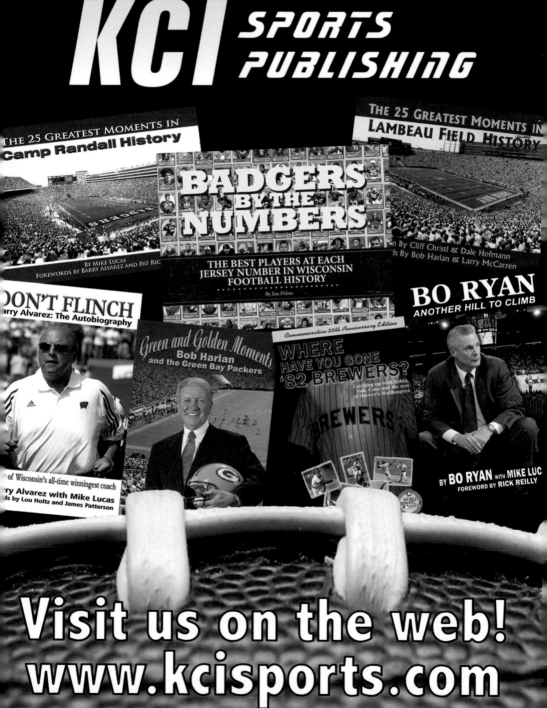